FLORIDA ORANGES

FLORIDA ORANGES

A Colorful History

ERIN THURSBY

AMERICAN PALATE

Published by American Palate
A Division of The History Press
Charleston, SC
www.historypress.com

Front and back cover images of oranges are released free of copyrights under Creative Commons CC0: https://pixabay.com/en/oranges-fruits-orange-tree-1117628; https://pxhere.com/en/photo/1152003. Front cover image of moving an orange tree at Flamingo Groves courtesy of Broward County Historical Archives, Hollywood (FL) Souvenir Collection. Back cover image of a postcard showing pickers at work in an Indian River Orange Grove (1898) courtesy of Detroit Publishing Company Collection, Library of Congress.

First published 2019

Manufactured in the United States

ISBN 9781467141192

Library of Congress Control Number: 2019943507

CONTENTS

ACKNOWLEDGEMENTS

Producing book would not have been possible without the help of many other people. Wendy J. Oliver at Dr. Phillips Charities; Elizabeth Kostecki, curator of Wray Home Museum/Historian; Erin Purdy, curator of the Broward County Historical Archive; Frank J. Johnson, executive director at West Volusia Historical Society; Brenda Burnette, Jim Ellis, Paul Meador, Stan Wood and many more, all of whom dedicated their time. The entire team at the Florida Collection desk of the Jacksonville Public Library were always an immense help, and they went above and beyond to get what this book needed. A final big thank-you for the support of my husband, Sean, and the Rock family.

AN ORANGE GROVE, NOT AN ORCHARD

Florida orange tree plantings go back five centuries. They are so ingrained in the culture of the state that many believe they're a native fruit. Even the very name we use to refer to groupings of cultivated oranges is a testament to that belief, for we call them "groves" and not "orchards."

Wherever the Native American population lived in Florida, oranges grew as well. The Seminoles got orange seeds through trade with the Spanish from the late 1500s through the mid-1800s, so the white settlers of the 1800s found groves already growing all over the state, ready to be thinned out and grafted with sweet oranges.

These copses of thin, sapling-like orange trees grew densely. This seemingly natural growth planted by the Seminoles is probably the reason why we call it a grove here in Florida. Today, the word *grove* can be nearly interchangeable with the word *orchard*. By the older, stricter definitions, an orchard is a planted or cultivated area of fruits or nuts, but a grove is wild—or at the very least less ordered. Californians will sometimes call it an orange orchard, which to any Floridian just sounds incredibly wrong.

Because the stands of orange trees were thought by some to be the result of nature—and, in any case, unorganized, not in neat rows like a traditional orchard—settlers called them groves. Even after white settlers cleared out dense parts, keeping the best trees for their rootstock, trees still weren't in rows, as farmers wouldn't move a good tree if they could help it (although they would sell some of the ones they moved for rootstock elsewhere). These early groves looked untamed, even when they weren't, and the implication

Citrus crate labels (which had their heyday sometime between 1920 and World War II) often featured Native Americans. 1932. *Brenda Eubanks Burnette personal collection.*

is that groves are more natural than orchards, something that's well in line with the marketing of the Florida orange, even as far back as the 1880s. The word *orchard* was sometimes used in the promotional pamphlets and books before 1900, but the word *grove* was used as well, eventually eclipsing *orchard*.

And so, *grove* became the word for any grouping of orange trees in Florida, even when growers set rows neatly. Usage of the word *grove* coupled with *orange* has spread far beyond the bounds of Florida. Most people in the United States at least, are far more likely to call an orange orchard a grove.

The vast majority of the groves grown by the Seminoles produced oranges of the sour or bitter kind, what the Spanish mainly grew in the early days, not sweet oranges. But even after the Seminoles got ahold of sweet seeds, those groves still tended not to be sweet. This is for two reasons. First, most of the sweet oranges from the 1500s through the early 1900s were not cold-hardy enough to survive, which is why growers learned to keep sour and bitter as the rootstock, grafting or budding on the sweet type to the tree. Secondly, growing from seed when it comes to oranges doesn't necessarily result in the fruit being the same as the parent, except in the case of a special mutation.

Orange seeds, as in most fruit, are the result of sexual reproduction in nature from cross-pollination, and each seed might have wildly different characteristics than the very orange it is inside. You might plant the seed and find this tree has thorns where the parent had none or bitter fruit where the parent was sweet. This is why, once a new and tasty orange was grown, the trees were valuable—growers used cuttings to propagate what are essentially clones, which can then be grafted or "budded" onto rootstock.

The sour oranges grown by the Spanish in the early 1500s were thought of as less culinary and more medicinal or essential, although that had changed by the end of the century, and oranges, sweet or sour, were becoming popular in Spanish beverages and cuisine. Sweet oranges were not unknown in the 1500s, and even though they had been cultivated in various parts of the world for centuries prior, their "discovery" by the Portuguese in the late 1400s spurred their popularity.

The real leap forward in orange cultivation for Florida came in the form of grafting or budding, a technique that firmly took hold by the first half of the 1800s. Even today, the budwood is taken from a proven sweet orange tree, tender shoots to be cut into the heartier rootstock. Most commercial concerns order budwood from a proven source.

Fifty years ago, the rootstock might have been sour orange, bitter orange or rough lemon, but growers, looking to stay ahead of all the latest diseases and problems plaguing citrus, seek resistant rootstocks. The Cleopatra Mandarin became popular years ago but is being replaced by less romantically named numbered rootstock from the Department of Agriculture and the Citrus Research and Education Center. A nursery might be maintained by the grower, but the seedling rootstock and budwood come from specialists who concentrate on producing them. Because of scourges such as greening, standards and laws for budwood are strict.

Once the sweet orange is budded onto the hardier rootstock, it's about another three to four years before the tree will bear anything worth harvesting. In the meantime, it's carefully nurtured—with plastic guards around the tender young tree to keep it from being nibbled at by wildlife.

The quality of the soil is measured and the precise fertilizer needed laid down every season to give a tree a good start in life. This is common practice today, but earlier growers weren't very scientific about fertilizer (if they fertilized at all), until by about the 1910s, when growers began measuring the characteristics of the soil and learning about what was needed to grow the best oranges and the biggest yield.

Today's trees are shorter than they were in 1890 or even 1960. This is by design. Growers come in with hedge croppers, with the top of all the orange trees in a grove uniformly trimmed and flattened, generally to no more than ten feet. Some prefer a more rounded natural shape, but most modern commercial growers keep their trees from growing up so much. It takes less energy for the tree to get water and nutrients to all its limbs because it doesn't have to work so much against gravity, and most importantly, if a freeze comes, it's a lot easier to cover the whole tree with water using micro-jets. These days, hardly anyone bothers with heaters in the grove, which were common through the 1900s, probably because of the rising cost of fuel—it isn't worth using them to save whole groves.

Lower trees also mean that they are easier to inspect for disease, although you'd need a ladder to reach their tops in most groves. Still, orange trees aren't thirty to one hundred feet tall today, and they're planted closer together than they used to be.

When Henry Sanford planted his experimental grove in the late 1800s, he had more than one hundred different varieties of oranges onsite. The 1800s and 1900s were a period of experimentation for growers, a veritable explosion of different types of oranges. Although we have some variety today (Navel, Hamlin, Pineapple, Ambersweet and Valencia being the most common), many orange types have been lost or are extremely difficult to find—such as the Lue Gim Gong and the Parson Brown. For the purposes of this book, an orange is anything that a consumer would consider an orange. A Satsuma, for instance, isn't really considered a true "sweet orange" in scientific circles since it's a Mandarin and not Citrus × sinensis.

There are plenty of dangers for a grower to worry over before and after the trees reach maturity. The one casting the darkest shadow these days is citrus greening. It threatens not only oranges but all citrus crops. The USDA has spent more than $250 million combating it. Citrus greening was found in Florida in 2005. Trees infected produce bitter, green and deformed fruit.

Greening is a bacterial infection of a tree, spread by Asian citrus psyllid and also through grafting. Because citrus greening infections progress slowly, and infected trees can produce marketable fruit for years, it affected production little by little. The total citrus harvest for Florida's 2011–12 growing season was 170.9 million boxes; over the next five years, it declined each year, and we had only 78 million boxes in 2016–17.

Citrus Research and Education Center has worked over the last decade with other agencies to research the problem, implementing disease-free nursery stock standards and educating growers on how to identify infection early and ways to control the Asian citrus psyllid with insecticides. As of 2018, the problem isn't solved, but CREC works to manage it, breed resistant trees and learn more about the disease.

Throughout the history of oranges in Florida, there have been many other problems for our growers to defeat—the earliest settlers had to worry about wars and attacks from Native Americans, in the late 1920s and '30s there were outbreaks of the Mediterranean fruit fly and citrus canker has been a worry throughout the 1900s, with the worst outbreak in the late 1990s and early 2000s. There have been many other scourges, from the mysterious spreading decline and black spot to all the pests and bugs wanting to take a bite out of citrus leaves and fruit. Growers today have to ensure that their tree is at the peak of health to fight off any disease, which means that the cost of keeping a tree healthy has gone up over the years.

Oranges aren't picked until ripe because, as with most citrus fruits, they do not continue to ripen after they are picked—they only ripen while on the tree. But not all of the fruit going to be juiced will even be orange. The skin color of an orange isn't always a measure of ripeness, and warm weather can cause an orange to turn green again. Inside, it might be perfectly delicious citrus perfection, but it doesn't always look the way you expect. This doesn't matter if the orange is juiced, but with gift-boxed oranges, appearance matters.

OLD ROOTS IN NORTHEAST FLORIDA

Although finding a grove in Northeast Florida these days is a difficult proposition, the first Florida orange tree blossomed somewhere around St. Augustine, brought in by the Spanish in the 1500s. We don't know for certain who buried that first seed, but most say that it was the famed explorer Juan Ponce de León, perhaps a rumor planted to give Florida oranges that extra dash of celebrity. Whatever the case, Spanish law in the sixteenth and seventeenth centuries required all ships bound for the Americas to have at least one hundred orange seeds on board, although later laws would require young trees aboard instead, as the long voyage often dried out the seeds. As soon as the sailors or settlers arrived, if there were any growing, they ate oranges to ward off scurvy.

It seems foolhardy today that oranges would be kept so far north in Florida as St. Augustine, and yet prior to 1835, oranges were grown even farther north in the Americas, along the Altamaha River in coastal Georgia and South Carolina. We should forgive our forebears their folly because all evidence from the time points to at least a century of warmth in the 1600s and 1700s. South Carolina had developed a taste for oranges after getting shipments of oranges from St. Augustine, but the state began expanding its production when a conflict between the English and the Spanish from 1739 to 1748 cut off supply. From November 1758 through November 1759, Charleston reportedly exported 418 barrels of oranges.

Even though oranges never became a big cash crop in South Carolina or Georgia, groves survived for much longer than current temperature patterns would suggest. Reports of old-growth trees indicate that the climate in these areas was warmer prior to 1835. It wasn't until the 1835 freeze that South Carolina and Georgia growers were fully discouraged.

EARLY GROWERS IN THE BRITISH PERIOD, 1763–83

Orange exports before the British Period were limited mainly to the eastern seaboard of North America, interrupted periodically by conflicts between Britain and Spain. By the 1760s, the English were intensely interested in all things exotic and were glad to have Florida supplying them with oranges. Transporting oranges across the Atlantic was a dicey proposition, but since there was profit to be made, and plenty of supply to do it with, British exporters perfected a process known as "wilting" to better help oranges survive the journey. It was done by spreading the oranges in direct sunlight, evaporating the excess moisture of the outer peel, which hardened the inner peel, protecting the fruit.

The word *orange* appears more than sixty times in William Bartram's account of east and west Florida in the 1770s *Bartram's Travels*. Bartram tells us that oranges were everywhere—in Indian encampments, on the banks of the St. Johns River and growing "wild" in thick stands—and Bartram ate them as he went, even using them in cooking to perk up food that had gone off a little: "As for provisions, I had saved one or two barbecued trout; the remains of my last evenings collection in tolerable good order, though the sultry heats of the day had injured them; yet by stewing them up afresh with the lively juice of Oranges, they served well enough for my supper."

The earliest true "orange baron" on record is the character Jesse Fish, who reportedly owned all of Anastasia Island, some ten thousand acres, as well as much of the city of St. Augustine. For historians, he's both intriguing and frustrating, as it is difficult to untangle the mythology of the man from the few known facts. Land speculator, con man, cuckold, entrepreneur, spy, savior and smuggler are all words or phrases that have been used to describe Fish.

William Bartram, a 1700s naturalist who traveled Florida, found oranges growing everywhere. *Engraved by T.B. Welch.*

Born in New York in the 1720s to a landowner with considerable holdings, he arrived at St. Augustine a British citizen between the age of ten and twelve in 1736 as a representative of the William Walton Company of New York, allowed to be there by the Spanish as a way to keep trade open. Fish acclimated well to his new home, learning Spanish from the Herreras, the prominent family who eventually saw him as one of their own. Fish was even described as more Spanish than British, absorbing the laws, customs and speech.

During the Seven Years' War, Fish helped smuggle provisions to the strapped St. Augustine from the British colonies, though as a British citizen, it was considered treason. Spain's supply lines were not enough to feed the city, so Fish found the profit worth the risk. For the starving citizens of St. Augustine in 1762, it made Fish a local hero. Like a lot of moneymakers of the time in Florida, his loyalties weren't with any country in particular—they were more local and monetary in nature.

In 1763, possession of Florida passed from the Spanish to the British, an opportunity that Fish did not allow to pass by without making a profit. He made a number of "off the books" deals that were highly illegal, agreeing to manage and hold land for the Spanish as a British citizen. Legally or not, he was the largest landowner in Florida by 1765.

Late in the 1760s, Fish became one of the first major exporters of oranges in Florida, exporting thousands of barrels through the 1780s. More than 65,000 Fish oranges arrived in London in the year 1776 to serve as the basis of orange shrub cocktails, which were apparently popular enough to drive up demand for the citrus. Other Floridian landowners, along with a Brit named James Hume, followed Fish's success. Hume planted some 3,500 sour oranges in the 1780s, as advised by Fish.

Following is an approximate re-creation of what an orange punch might have been like over in jolly old England when Jesse Fish was most heavily exporting his oranges in the late 1770s. The alcoholic shrub base is not the non-alkie vinegar version that's better known today. Gin was probably the most popular spirit, but they also had access to rum and whiskey. It's likely they mixed alcohol, sugar and orange juice up in a concentrated dose for preservation, which they would later add to other ingredients. Jason Gustavson, local St. Augustine bar manager of Prohibition Kitchen, has formulated an updated version for your tasting pleasure.

Jesse Fish Shrub Punch

1.5 ounces Shrub (recipe below)
0.5 ounce PX Sherry
2.5 ounces Earl Grey Tea

Shake aggressively for a few seconds and serve over ice with mint and an orange wheel.

Shrub Recipe

Peel or zest (no pith) 8 large oranges and add to 1 cup of sugar. Use a muddler to smash the orange peels into the sugar to express all the oils from the skin. Do this process off and on for about 30 minutes. Take a 750ml bottle of clear rum and add to sugar/orange and stir until all sugar has dissolved. Store in an airtight container and let sit for 3 days. After the resting period, add ¾ cup of water and stir again. The shrub can now sit in the fridge for 4 to 6 months with the peels still on the mix. You only need to strain the peels when making a cocktail.

When the British gave over control of the colonies to the newly formed United States of America in 1783, the Americans ceded Florida over to Spain because of Spanish support during the Revolutionary War. As the Spanish came back, Fish had to settle his many accounts, and by the late 1780s, he was claiming that he was in serious debt and owned very little land, some of which was due to mismanagement from a relative by marriage he'd asked to be his agent. By his death in 1790, all that remained was his El Vergel estate.

Although every backyard and courtyard in Northeast Florida seemed to feature at least one citrus tree in the 1600s and 1700s, it took three hundred years after the 1500s introduction from the Spanish before oranges became a true industry in the area, with the exception of a few early growers such as Fish.

But their example, and the wild groves seeded by the Native Americans all over Florida, inspired others in the beginning of the nineteenth century. One of them was the legendary Zephaniah Kingsley, who owned land in and around Northeast Florida. Today, you can tour one of those pieces of land at Kingsley Plantation.

THE PLANTATION ERA, 1800–1860

Born in 1765 in Bristol, England, Zephaniah Kingsley was brought to South Carolina by his merchant father when he was just five years old. Kingsley Sr. had gone broke in England. He had enough left to try to change his fortunes, but revolution was brewing in the colonies and his staunchly English loyalties left his family in the lurch. Early in the conflict, Kingsley's father was smart enough to remain absent during particular times of strife, returning when the revolution had come back to more of a simmer and less of a boil, and then buying up seized property as the war drove down prices. But by the 1780s, the young Zephaniah saw his father's property taken and the elder Kingsley thrown in jail several times, as a result of his declared loyalty to the Crown. They would later move to New Brunswick in Canada.

Learning the lessons of his father's loyalty, the younger Zephaniah would swear oaths to many nations over his lifetime. Zephaniah Kingsley Jr. went where the opportunities were and swore whatever oaths necessary so he could do business—first swearing an oath of allegiance to the Americans in 1793 so he could trade at Charlestown and then acting as a sea captain in 1798 from the base of St. Thomas, where he swore another oath to the Dutch. Looking for more profit, he spent time as the captain of a slave ship in the early 1800s, and in 1803, he swore a third oath of allegiance, this time to the Spanish in St. Augustine, near his new base of operations, Laurel Grove.

By 1811, Zephaniah Kingsley made a handsome sum of $10,000 one year from his Laurel Grove plantation (about $170,500 in modern money), some of which came from his orange grove of more than seven hundred Mandarin orange trees, although he grew a number of other cash crops, including cotton and grains. Laurel Grove was found near Doctors Lake and the St. Johns River, south of Jacksonville in present-day Orange Park. Most plantations had a grove and made money from it—or they just grew oranges for themselves—but it didn't tend to be their sole source of income.

Three years later, Kingsley left Laurel Grove for Kingsley Plantation on Fort George Island, where he also planted oranges, reaping the benefits over the next ten years. Most of what the Kingsleys grew on Fort George was cotton, but Kingsley Plantation featured a mix of crops, and although oranges were present, they were a much smaller part of the picture than they had been at Laurel Grove.

The reason the Kingsley family abruptly left the profitable Laurel Grove for the Fort George Island is an interesting bit of history and a snapshot of the unrest landholders had to endure. In 1811–13, the United States attempted to annex Northeast Florida in a covert conflict called the Patriot War. Among other concerns, the United States government was unhappy about Spain's policy of allowing runaway slaves to cross the border and encouraging communities of freedmen to flourish just a few days from the border of Georgia. Spain's position on slavery was that it wasn't a permanent state of being, but that a slave could buy his freedom. Spain also did not fully curtail Native American activities and did use them as shock troops during the Patriot War, one of many factors that led into First Seminole War just after this conflict.

The American "Patriots" attacked isolated plantations such as Laurel Grove, killing some slaves and freemen and capturing others for enslavement in the United States. By this point, Kingsley had again sworn oaths both to the U.S. and Spanish governments. Some of the Laurel Grove slaves also ended up being killed by the Seminoles hired out by the Spanish. Formerly, Kingsley had maintained good relations with the Native Americans, but as he supplied goods throughout the war to the U.S. forces, and because the "Patriots" had captured Laurel Grove as a stronghold, the natives attacked.

To the Spanish afterward, he maintained that he had been forced to work with the Americans. When he was in his seventies, he claimed that he had been coerced and cooperated for fear of losing his property, but he did also use the support given to the Patriots as political leverage when appealing to American authorities. In any case, for much of the conflict, Kingsley wasn't even present at Laurel Grove, leaving things in the capable hands of his black freed wife, Anna Kingsley.

Anna Kingsley ultimately showed where her loyalty lay. By 1913, the plantation had become a base of operations for the less lawful elements of the American side, and Anna hadn't had word from Zephaniah for quite a while. While the Americans were there, she managed to keep safe the majority of the slaves and children by hiding some of them in the woods nearby, and when the Spanish came with gunboats, chasing the marauders to the Laurel Grove base, she got on the Spanish boat using a canoe and a password. She told the commander on board about the state of the fortifications, number of men and how the Americans had temporarily abandoned the plantation because of the cannon fire. The commander questioned her loyalty to the Spanish when he saw the marauding forces lurking in the woods nearby, suspecting that she had set them up for an ambush. She denied it and looked for the first chance to prove her loyalty. When it was mentioned to her that the unoccupied, mostly ruined (but fortified) plantation could be a base of

An engraving of the more well-known Kingsley Plantation, where Zephaniah, Anna and the Kingsley family moved after Anna burned down Laurel Grove in 1813. *Florida Memory Project, #PR10577.*

operations and a source of food for the U.S. forces, Anna Kingsley burned Laurel Grove to the ground, as well as the five-acre plot in her own name just across the water.

We know Kingsley today for his progressive ideas on slavery, though in truth, they were only better by comparison than the crueler gang system. He allowed the slaves on his land to make their own profit after the day's work was through, using the task system, something that was actually fairly common to the Northeast Florida area. This was not borne entirely out of benevolence, but rather the desire to get more and better quality work from his slaves, who would also be less likely to revolt. Although he did speak up for the rights of freed blacks, he still traded in human beings and defended the institution of slavery itself as necessary, while making a healthy profit from it. Kingsley married a number of his slaves (he practiced polygamy, and Anna Kingsley was just fourteen when she had her first child by him), and he produced many interracial children. The Spanish were more tolerant of mixed-race families than those in the United States. As Kingsley was concerned about the rights of Anna and his children in the future (and because the Seminole conflicts with the Americans were making the area less stable and less profitable), he left the Florida orange growing behind him in the 1830s after control passed from the Spanish to the United States.

Any plantation owner or orange grower through the 1860s—in addition to scale bugs, rot, freezes and the instability of the local governance—also had American Indians to consider. Florida land owners ran the risk of being attacked by the natives, who would sometimes raid and destroy plantations, most notably during the Second Seminole War from 1835 to 1842. Most of the true battles happened in North Central and Southwest Florida during this time, but the natives did sometimes strike in the Northeast. One of the more memorable attacks was an 1841 raid on a plantation known as the "Mandarin Massacre." Only four whites lost their lives in the Mandarin Massacre—a babe-in-arms, a woman and two men—but the attack and the isolated nature of these plantations did frighten landowners and families nearby, who hid in the swamp until the natives had left. Besides the loss of life, the natives also slaughtered hogs and destroyed a grove of oranges.

The Spanish always had their problems with the Native Americans but had largely given them free rein in places outside their control because it was too much trouble and too costly to do otherwise. When the United States took over in 1821, the government had different ideas about that arrangement, which led to fresh conflict and the Second Seminole War about fourteen years later. The Second Seminole War cost the U.S. government an estimated $15 million. Even though there were still Native Americans in the state afterward, the Armed Occupation Act passed by Congress in 1842 pushed a small boom in land claims, as it provided free land to settlers (a precursor to the Homestead Act) who defended it for five years and cleared 5 acres of the 160 acres they could claim; more than one thousand people did so claim from 1842 to 1843.

Whether one would be attacked sometimes depended on the relationship of the planter with the local natives. If a planter traded regularly with them and treated them with respect, chances were that they would not be raided. But tribes were by no means unified, and kind treatment of one group didn't mean that a planter would be safe from another, especially if you left your groves unattended.

ORANGE FEVER BETWEEN THE WAR AND THE FREEZE, 1865–95

The real boom time for citrus in Northeast Florida was undoubtedly later, between the Civil War and the Big Freeze, when the state was finally stable enough for such enterprises. The Civil War halted the burgeoning citrus exports from Florida almost completely, as the Union and the Confederacy traded strategic parts of the state back and forth. The Union captured and abandoned Jacksonville several times during the war. There wasn't really any point in growing or building anything during those four years, first because supply lines weren't stable and second because as the soldiers left they would destroy anything of use to their enemy. Oranges survived mainly because there were so many of them lining the St. Johns River and because simply chopping them down didn't tend to work, as illustrated by the Englishman Sir Francis Drake's earlier efforts to leave Spanish St. Augustine orangeless. Drake had all the orange trees of St. Augustine chopped down when he sacked the city in 1586, but he didn't kill them to the ground, so the stumps tenaciously grew new shoots and those trees bore fruit once again. So while Civil War troops destroyed a state-of-the-art steam-powered sawmill in Arlington (today a suburb of Jacksonville), trees still stood or had regrown. Not all of them, but enough to rootstock to seed hope when the war ended in 1865.

Despite little freezes in the 1880s, books and pamphlets on the subject of oranges still brimmed with enthusiasm. It would be work, yes, but there was a fortune to be made. More than that, they claimed that oranges were a stable, steady income. In Helen Harcourt's *Florida Fruits and How to Raise Them*, published in 1886, she asserted that "no one who owns a grove at the present day will live to see its decay." The fame of oranges, she said, "is not built upon a sandy foundation, but upon a gold-bearing rock, and such it shall stand forevermore."

Reverend T.W. Moore's 1881 handbook on oranges touted enormous dividends on the very first page: "When compared to the profit from other kinds of business, that derived from orange-growers is so large that a statement of facts is often withheld because the truth seems fabulous to those who have only had experience with other kinds of fruit."

What both books and many of the promotional pamphlets and articles of the day had in common are reassurances to objections any orange investor might have, with tales of fantastic earnings sprinkled in between. Both declare that the limited geographic area where oranges are grown mean that the supply will never exceed the demand. Orange fever, by the 1880s, was so publicized that some investors believed that they might be too late or that all the farmers would glut the market so much that prices would fall.

As a lot of promotional writers did at the time, Reverend Moore dealt directly with the issue of freezes—first, he cleared up the perception that there is a frostline at all, saying that whole state can experience frost, and then, after establishing this piece of forthrightness and honesty, he noted that frost is good for the trees: "I am sure my own orange trees were never so free from insects and in so healthy condition as to-day, eight months after the frost of December 1880."

These books mixed marketing and practical tips for a farmer new to the business, and while they could be useful, there was self-interest on the part of some of the writers, even if their business wasn't land speculation. More people coming to grow meant more land sold, which would increase their own property values and bring more money to the area. And like most folks on the edge of a financial bubble, they really did believe that the good times were never going to end.

HARRIET BEECHER STOWE AND THE MAKING OF MANDARIN

Religion and the civil rights of newly freed slaves were most definitely intertwined with the promotion of the Florida by eager northerners and, by extension, the riches that oranges could bring. Some of this was driven by reform politics. Since Florida wasn't yet widely populated, an influx of northerners could outvote the more prejudiced southerners, ensuring black education and, in time, voting rights.

Harriet Beecher Stowe wasn't the typical orange grower in the state, but she certainly was one of the most well known beyond the borders of Florida. Although she did get income from her oranges, there were no more than approximately 120 trees on her property. Still, her articles on Florida and on oranges influenced many of those who came to the state. Today, we remember her for her seminal *Uncle Tom's Cabin*, but her postwar *Palmetto Leaves* was also a bestseller. This collection of essays on the joys of Florida living in Mandarin, and her articles in the *Christian Union* and other newspapers of the day, had a tremendous impact on the northern settlement of Florida. It can be argued that her articles in the *Union* had even more of an audience than *Palmetto Leaves*, as its reported subscription number was eighty-one thousand in 1872, most of them being upper-class New Yorkers.

An abolitionist with deep roots in religion, Stowe and her husband helped found a church in Mandarin, and in article after article, she tirelessly promoted the state, even as she dispelled mythologies that might disappoint the vacationer. "Florida," she wrote in *Palmetto Leaves*, "like a piece of embroidery, has two sides to it—one side all tag-rag and thrums, without order or position; and the other side showing flowers and arabesques and brilliant coloring."

Harriet Beecher Stowe. *National Archives and Records Administration, NAID, 535784.*

The lure of her celebrity and the impact on winter tourism and oranges cannot be overstated. Many of these northern tourists were also there to scout land prospects and were quick to catch orange fever. Interest in her was so pronounced that the *New York Tribune* sent a reporter, a sort of early paparazzo of prose, who minutely described every inch of their property, down to what the cracks behind their wallpaper were caulked with. Stowe responded with annoyed humor, writing, "We cut out the article and kept it in our pocket, and whenever we were at fault about the length and breadth of a room, the height and thickness of a board, there we had it." In a biography of Stowe, written by one of her sons and a grandson after her death, they related that "[a]n enterprising steamboat company in Jacksonville advertised excursions to Mandarin and Mrs. Stowe's orange grove—so much for the round trip—without consulting her, or offering consideration of any sort for being made a public spectacle." Even so, the Stowe family was as welcoming as they could be, barring damage to their orange trees, which tourists occasionally caused. Stowe and her family eventually came to an arrangement with the steamboats and the tourists, sometimes even holding cookouts for the crowd, along with meet-and-greets for a modest fee.

On the subject of oranges, while Stowe did warn that some years a freeze would take the crop, she posited that "apart from the danger of frost, the orange-crop is the most steady and certain of any known fruit." She brushed off other dangers from the scale-bug, saying, "Nothing has been seen of it in an epidemic form for many years, and growers now have no apprehensions from this source."

Stowe wrote not just about her little patch of property and the neighbors surrounding but also about other points of interest in Florida, such as Jacksonville, St. Augustine, travel down the St. Johns River and even a tour of Silver Springs by torchlight.

In writing about Magnolia, a boardinghouse near Green Cove Springs, she mentioned a lack of sweet orange groves on that side of the river saying, "The oranges about the house are entirely of the wild kind.... Formerly there were extensive orange-groves, with thousands of bearing trees....The frost of 1835 killed the trees and they have never been reset. Oranges are not, therefore, either cheap or plenty at Magnolia or Green Cove. Nothing shows more strikingly the want of enterprise that has characterized this country than this. Seedling oranges planted the very next day after the great frost would have been bearing ten years after, and would, ere now yielded barrels and barrels of fruit.... One would have thought so very simple and easy a measure would have been adopted."

Now a neighborhood of Jacksonville, Mandarin, where Stowe wintered from 1867 to 1884, gets its name from a variety of orange. It was the name that stuck. Prior to that, it was San Antonio when the Spanish had it, anglicized to San Anthony when the British knew it and then briefly as Monroe in honor of the president when the United States acquired the territory in 1821. First mention of the current name came about 1830, so even as early as that, settlers cultivated groves or, at the very least, promoted them—enough that by 1835, when the hard freeze came, it did lose some residents their livelihood there, and even farther south in Green Cove Springs, where Stowe had noted the abandoned groves.

CHRISTIANS AND ORANGES IN ARLINGTON

Arlington was also one of the major orange growing neighborhoods in the Jacksonville area between 1865 and 1900. Geographically, its slightly elevated land made it unusual for North Florida and a good proposition for oranges, both because of good drainage and because higher ground often did better than low-lying areas without air circulation. The neighborhood on a map today is a large one, largely going from the St. Johns River to the Intracoastal Waterway and, in one place, all the way to the Atlantic Ocean. But at this time, most of the orange growing and the settlements were right along the banks of the St. Johns River.

From about 1870 through the 1890s, Arlington became part of the winter home and resort movement of Florida. A number of religious-based communities sprang from the resort movement. These weren't cults or compounds, but real estate promoters marketed Arlington to Christians as a winter retreat surrounded by like-minded residents with a church where they could worship.

William Matthews formed the Arlington Bluff Association, which sought out Christian buyers of all denominations. The isolation of Arlington was a selling point, but it was also a drawback; so, as an enticement for northerners, the association gave residents access to the nearby Jacksonville, furnishing a steamer that took four daily trips. Matthews's other major endeavors were the profitable orange groves that surrounded his estate in Arlington.

His groves, like the others in North Florida, withered in the Great Freeze of 1894–95, succumbing completely in 1899. The series of '94–'95 freezes, known colloquially as the "Big One," still loom large in the historical memories of Florida orange growers. By this time, the commercial orange business had grown up quite a bit since the colder freeze of 1835 and the smaller freezes in the 1880s. A far greater number of growers felt the economic impact of the disaster. Since so many had been told that oranges were a sure investment, plenty of these folks had sunk their entire farms and fortunes into their groves, whereas in the 1800s through 1830s, orange growers were a little more likely to grow other crops and have other enterprises, such as cattle or cotton.

The freeze was bad enough that there are accounts of growers all over the state, after seeing the damage, just getting up from breakfast, leaving the meal on the table, locking the doors and never coming back again. Other accounts say that fixing breakfast wasn't possible—the eggs were frozen solid.

The uneven onslaught of cold weather was another factor; a second freeze in 1895 would happen just as trees weakened from the previous 1894 freeze were beginning to recover. Farmers would look back on the Big One as the measure of the worst freeze for nearly a century.

The freezes didn't just kill the majority of orange trees in Northeast Florida; they also froze the winter tourism market and the land speculation that came with it. The death of citrus made property values plummet, and with the railway expanding ever-southward, finally completed all the way down to Key West by 1912, it seemed like everyone was moving south.

DR. GARNETT'S GROVES, 1880–1940s

While the late 1890s freezes discouraged many of the growers in Northeast Florida, and the hard freezes that followed in the next decade convinced most that they should move south or find another occupation, there was a man in the St. Augustine area who stood his ground and diversified. His name was Dr. Reuben B. Garnett, and he opted not just to count on the oranges for his profit, but rather count on the people who would want to see them.

He planted Dr. Garnett's Grove in the 1880s, but it became a tourist attraction later, from the 1900s through the 1940s—first operated by the man himself, then by family members and then by local entrepreneur Walter B. Fraser, who eventually stripped it of the Garnett name, although it was still known to locals by that name. Fraser dubbed it the "Oldest Orange Grove" and, for a time, the "Orange Blossom Stable." At the time, Fraser was also owner of the Fountain of Youth and the Oldest School House.

When Dr. Garnett ran the grove, he planted pecan trees, replanted oranges after the devastation of the 1899 freeze and installed a photographer and photography studio there. There were postcards and mementos aplenty, which were a bit of a novelty in the early 1900s.

What Garnett and later owners were actually selling wasn't orange juice or oranges—it was an idea of old Florida, in a place where people came to buy it: St. Augustine. From a *St. Augustine Record* story reminiscing about the land: "It was probably everybody's idea of what rural Florida should look like—only with city conveniences near. Centuries-old live oaks with hanging Spanish moss shaded roadways, a double row of Washingtonia robusta palms offered a scenic vista. Orange trees covered the property."

Dr. Garnett died in 1922, and his daughter and her family kept the attraction open. They added a few more points of interest besides the grove tour and pictures, including a stable and horseback rides, as well as a glass blowing studio. They provided horseback riding lessons and a riding ring, and you could even ride across town to St. Augustine Beach.

Through the 1950s and 1960s, bit by bit, development consumed the now-closed Garnett's groves—U.S. 1 was rerouted through part of the property, the Garnett House was demolished in '54 and, in 1962, the last of the live oaks were bulldozed for a Holiday Inn, Winn-Dixie and gas station on the new Ponce de Leon Boulevard. But the final blow to the property was in 1973, when developers built a motel on the San Marco Avenue end of the old grove.

UNSUNG HEROES OF THE GROVE

Picking an orange still takes people power, and there's a definite cultural division between those who manage farms and those who pick the oranges.

SANFORD'S LABOR ISSUES OF THE 1800s

In 1870, Henry Sanford—or at least the managers he hired—were looking for labor to clear the land for what would become Sanford's Belair and St. Gertrude Groves. The engineering firm Whitner and Marks, in charge of getting the groves up and running, found it difficult to keep staff. Mr. J.N. Whitner attempted to use Florida Crackers (defined at the time as generationally white Floridians whose ancestors originally settled during the English colonial era, many of whom lived off the land), but after a rough start, he opted to recruit a black workforce. This proved untenable because the white workers, who had been fired for laziness and incompetence, resented the African Americans being brought in to replace them, and the local Ku Klux Klan stoked that resentment. Guns were shot off, bullets wounding some in the camp. Whitner and Marks set guards around the camp, appealing to the law-abiding citizens in the area. This helped calm down the violence, but not long after, Sanford's mill was attacked and the black labor force there driven from the city.

The threat of violence against his workers is likely why Sanford quickly decided on importing Swedish labor. True, they were foreign, but given the color of their skin, they were far less likely to provoke the ire of the Klansmen. The immigrants arrived with nearly nothing—even the clothes on their backs were substandard.

Slavery no longer held sway in the South after the Civil War, but indentured servitude was another thing entirely. Sanford paid for their passage over, plus their room and board, in return for at least a year's worth of labor. An overseer of Sanford's had mistakenly promised them along the way that Sanford would provide clothing, shoes and bedding for them, and although Sanford wasn't legally obligated to provide these, he did so to avoid ill feeling. He also gave them a weekly credit at the store he owned in return for extending their contract for a longer period of time.

Sanford's manager, Henry DeForest, said that the Swedes were being treated well enough, even if it was hard work. Still, Swedes unable to adjust to the Florida heat did die. Even so, some workers wrote to friends to get them to sign contracts as well; others asked for a loan to extend their service in order to bring their wives over. But there were runaways and a strike for more than one day off during the Christmas season.

Many of the Swedes were not satisfied with their treatment or the amount of rations, especially those that Sanford had "hired out." He'd imported too many Swedes for the work, and he loaned some to other farmers, taking half or all of the money for their labor.

The Swede experiment ended within two years, and Sanford went back to black labor. The troubles with the white population began again, with a party of armed men twice visiting the camp, telling the black labor force to leave before there was trouble. The police were not very much help, as one of the armed men had actually been the sheriff. DeForest turned toward the marshals instead, and when one of his black laborers was badly beaten, DeForest signed an arrest warrant to bring them to justice. DeForest was undeterred, even when he himself began receiving threats of harm should any other arrests be made. Eventually, the group making trouble accepted that a black labor force was needed for citrus, but it would not be the last time the Ku Klux Klan would be involved in a labor dispute.

MARTHA MICKENS AT CROSS CREEK

One of the most detailed accounts of the relationship between a small grower and the workers tending oranges has to be in the pages of Marjorie Kinnan Rawlings's *Cross Creek*, a largely autobiographical account of times spent at her Alachua farm, which included a small grove on the property, mainly during the Great Depression.

Rawlings almost exclusively hired black folks. The main help she looked to hire was a couple to live in the tenant home on the grounds—a woman to be her maid to help with cooking and cleaning and a man to manage the orange groves. Once, under social pressure, she gave in and hired a white couple to do the job, saying, "I was told in the village again and again that it was not fair to the unemployed there to pay my comparatively high wages to Negroes, when white men were hungry." As the KKK was active in Florida, as lightly as she treated it in her book, the pressure was probably more than just social and carried with it an implied threat.

As she was needing help again and the word had gone out, a white man named Lum came to her, probably with the backing of the town, insisting that she hire him and his wife as at the moment she was between grove handlers and maids. As she said, "They descended on me against my protests." The maid worked out quite well, but Lum was a different story. "The job was an appalling blow to Lum. To keep up with the routine work meant from eight to ten full hours a day. He could not believe it."

When the mercury dropped, black hands were rounded up for a grove firing, along with wood and kerosene, to keep fires burning inside the grove and hold the winter temperatures at bay. From Rawlings's account:

> *The work is so cruel that it seems to me the least I can do is take care of the men properly. We had pounds of hamburg, baked beans, bread and butter, jams, relishes, sweet buns and hot coffee, and the men came in relays of two through the night to eat and warm themselves by the roaring wood range in the kitchen. I had also served quarts of gin and whiskey, and I suspect that this heating medium is the source of my success in getting hands for firing. I turned the liquor over to Lum with instructions to parcel it out through the night as the men needed it. Authority and liquor went to Lum's head. He drank the lion's share and toward morning, while the men shivered and did without, Lum was overcome and returned to his bed to sleep in drunken comfort.*

When the second day came, Lum simply refused to work, and Rawlings was saved the trouble of letting him go. He said that the job was too much for him, too hard and too much work, so Rawlings sent him back to town, telling him to spread the word that "the job out here is a man's job." She thought he must have done well, as the protests against her continuing to

Martha Mickens with Marjorie Kinnan Rawlings. *Marjorie Kinnan Rawlings, Special and Area Studies Collections, George A. Smathers Libraries, University of Florida, Gainesville, Florida.*

Martha Mickens and her husband, Old Will. *Marjorie Kinnan Rawlings, Special and Area Studies Collections, George A. Smathers Libraries, University of Florida, Gainesville, Florida.*

hire a black grove manager instead of a white one were no longer spoken of when she went to town.

Her lodestar between the times when she did not have help was an older black woman named Martha, who filled in with the maid's work but who also served as a kind of hiring boss to recommend and get Rawlings help for the grove when she needed it, mainly in the form of her extensive brood of grown children and their husbands.

Martha Mickens introduced herself when Rawlings came to Cross Creek, saying, "Me and my man, Old Will was the first hands on this place....We too old now to do steady work, but I just wants to tell you, any time you gets in a tight, us is here to do what we can." She was as good as her word, filling in or finding someone to fill in whenever any of her daughters or maids could not work due to illness or pregnancy or, in the case of the men, suddenly went off drinking. Martha's knowledge of rural ways over the years—whether it be poultry, cows, gardening or citrus—proved valuable to Rawlings again and again.

The pickers and the grove firers worked for Rawlings on a more temporary basis. She gave an account of the dexterity needed to pick in her groves:

> *My trees are old and tall and thirty foot ladders must be used to reach the tops. Only an experienced hand can manage one alone. He runs to his tree with it, balancing it like a juggling acrobat. The tall ladders rest precariously against the frail topmost branches, but the pickers mount quickly and surely.*

One picker in particular, called "Preacher," was one of the best to come to her grove—"his hands swift as the claws of the hawk among the oranges." Often he led them in song, singing old spirituals and preaching as they picked. When the Preacher was absent, they sang the songs of the juke joints; "Shake that Thing" was apparently one of the most popular.

We see this world and workers through the eyes of Rawlings, a white writer and grower of time—worth reading, but if you'd like a black perspective from that era, Zora Neal Hurston's writings on Florida are a good place to start, in particular on the Ocoee Massacre in 1920. This event chased all the African Americans out of this Florida town, and although it was connected to voting rights, control of black labor by blacks was certainly a factor.

KKK AND THE ORANGE UNION

While the overseers and foremen were sometimes white, it seems that many of the pickers were black through the 1940s. Grove workers and race relations were inextricably linked, so in racially charged Florida, there was bound to be trouble.

Government work programs during the Depression set working conditions and pay. Many industries partnered with the government to get workers, but they had to abide by government-mandated standards for wages and conditions. Workers in citrus pushed for the industry to be a part of the programs, but the growers did not agree.

Wooden sorters such as these were used to sort citrus by size in Bakers County. *Glen St. Mary Nursery Collection.*

Packinghouse workers wrap each orange in tissue paper. *Glen St. Mary Nursery Collection.*

At the time, growers had gotten very good at meeting the supply—so good that they had oversupplied, and the price per orange was down. Quality control at the time wasn't as stringent, another reason prices weren't as high as they should have been. And of course, the Great Depression was happening.

Workers began to unionize and organize in Polk County, much to the consternation of the growers, who felt they couldn't afford a bump in pay and conditions. As the workforce was largely African American, growers turned to a well-known organization for help: the Ku Klux Klan.

The growers raised standards and pay just a touch to placate the workers. That—and the disappearance of a major union organizer who had been picked up by what looked to be law enforcement but was never seen or heard from again—was enough to dissolve the union.

Whether the majority of workers were black depended on the county—in far North Florida Baker County, for instance, all the nursery workers employed (through the 1930s at least) were white, while the turpentine still workers in the area were all black. Grove overseers tended to be white, but the workforce was generally all one color or another rather than mixed.

HILLARD BARON OF FROSTPROOF

In McPhee's oft-cited book, *Oranges*, an account of his Florida travels and talks with orange men of the 1960s, Ben Hill Griffin Jr. gave credit where credit was due as they flew over his land in a helicopter:

> *"There's where we started," Griffin shouted, pointing towards a block of trees. "Right yonder, on that ten acres. I planted all of that next grove, too. Forty acres. I grew the rootstock in my backyard. I had a colored man lived on the original ten. Hillard Baron. He had one hand, and half of one foot was gone, but he cleared that second forty acres. Felled big oaks. If I had a hundred men like Hillard, I could conquer the state of Florida."*

The date of Griffin's start was 1933, when his father gave him those first ten acres, so Hillard likely worked for Griffin sometime between 1933 and the 1950s. That he was missing a hand and part of a foot was probably an advantage during World War II, as that made Hillard ineligible for service in the military.

The fact was, there were more than a hundred men and women like Hillard (although very few were probably missing as many of their limbs) who helped white farmers in Florida conquer and care for citrus land. From a pamphlet on Marion County agriculture probably published in the 1920s or '30s, the labor of the day was described this way: "Ordinary labor here as elsewhere in the South is mostly Negro. Wages vary from $1.25–2.50 a day...the number of white employees on farms and in the groves is increasing, particularly since the introduction of the tractor and other modern machinery."

Picking isn't easy work. Under the U.S. Secretary of Labor's plan to reduce unemployment during the twentieth century, they sent unemployed people to places where there was demand, sending busloads of workers to Florida during the orange picking season, but nearly all of those quit. One of the workers even wrote to the Florida State Employment Service, "In one half day, I have learned that I am not a citrus picker. If you know of any seasonal farm work in the state that doesn't require the combined agility of a monkey and the stamina of a horse, I would like to hear of it."

THE BAHAMIAN WAVE

Native labor, even from the black community, wasn't always easy to get. In South and Central Florida, particularly during the 1940s and '50s, growers recruited Bahamians to do the work. An estimated thirty thousand Bahamian men and women migrated temporarily to the United States as agricultural labor between 1943 and 1965.

Conditions for the workers varied greatly—they could be living in a house with their family, in tents or in outbuildings, but most often they would be housed in camps with hundreds of others—as in the Okeechobee Farm Labor Supply Center in Belle Glade, Florida. In July 1943, the center housed 850 Bahamian workers.

Dr. Philip Phillips of Orange County made use of these workers, and to ensure that he had help whenever he needed it in his vast groves, he hired many of them for the year instead of seasonally, and a small village grew up around his eighteen square miles of grove. While many growers simply used the seasonal help, Phillips saw the wisdom of taking care of his workers, establishing a hospital in the 1950s to provide healthcare for black folk. On a practical level, the benefits like the liquor Rawlings offered

Living quarters and "juke joint" for migratory workers, a slack season at Belle Glade. 1944. *Library of Congress, Prints and Photographs Division.*

during overnight grove firings, or the healthcare Phillips provided, were a way to ensure getting a workforce when they were needed most. And the year-round pay also made a job with Phillips more desirable for workers, so that Phillips didn't have to work so hard to recruit in an emergency, such as when a grove needed firing or the crop needed to come down quickly ahead of a frost warning.

In a 1999 interview, Broward County resident Dorothy McIntyre (who was more than sixty at the time) recalled the workers' city of the late 1940s as partially tents, but that they "had wooden buildings" with "barricades like the Army had" and that the bathhouse was separate. McIntyre's mother used to cook for the men who lived out of those barracks. The workers were black Bahamians. McIntyre's father came from the Bahamas under what she and many other Bahamians called "LaContract," as labor in the Orlando area. It was called this because each worker signed a contractual agreement to work in the United States as part of the British West Indies Labor Program.

From an oral history recording, workers described the hazards of working in Wabasso near Vero Beach. There were mosquitoes—"you could rake your hand…and grab a handful of them…we had [to] smoke the trees with the tractor while we pick the fruit." And when the cold came, "when you get out there in an hour or two, you don' feel like you had no toes."

IMMIGRATION ISSUES

What might be startling to most outside observers is how much modern growers value the workers and how pro-immigration they are. They've seen firsthand what a boon to the industry immigrants can be, and frankly, they need the labor. Stan Wood of Southeast Florida has grown up in the citrus industry and horticulture since the 1940s, helping to manage the groves at Flamingo Gardens (which today are no longer there, and he got out of the business in the late '80s). He's seen the workforce change as immigration laws have shifted, from Bahamian to Jamaican to Mexicans and South Americans.

Said Wood, "The same conversations we're having now about letting them in, we had fifteen years ago, and we're going to probably have again." He's all for legalizing and legitimizing the workers if only for the massive tax dollars those workers can bring in. If the country had better laws to allow them legally, he reasons, we'd increase the tax base by millions.

A migrant orange picker in Polk County. 1944. *Library of Congress, Prints and Photographs Division.*

For the past few years, commercial grower Paul Meador at his Southwest groves near LaBelle, Florida, has relied on a visa guest worker program called H-2A. Part of the deal is advertising to ensure that the jobs haven't been taken from Americans, but Meador said that "it's been a decade since we've had a domestic American even apply." The regulated program requires that Meador pay his workers about eleven to twelve dollars per hour, and he incentivizes with a bonus based on the amount picked. In times past, they were paid solely by amount they picked. The average amount Meador pays is about sixteen to eighteen dollars per hour, plus free housing and transportation. "It's a great deal for us, and a great deal for them," said Meador.

Every once in a while, some scientist proclaims that he or she has fashioned a decent mechanical picker, but thus far, nothing has been good enough for most farmers. Some of these old pickers used hurricane-force winds, stripping the trees not just of the fruit but also of all the leaves. This is a problem when it comes to Valencias because one tree can have fruit of varying ripeness. Canopy shakers are too indiscriminate to be worthwhile. Any viable mechanical picker would have to recognize what was ripe and what wasn't. There have been mechanical pickers with Artificial Intelligence built in to judge ripeness, but they haven't yet been able to match a human. Although Meador has used mechanical pickers in the past when labor was hard to get, nothing beats the discerning eye and gentle touch of a good citrus worker.

A SMALL RESURGENCE IN THE PANHANDLE

The Panhandle and Northwest Florida aren't especially known for orange groves. Early orange experiments happened in the Carolinas and Georgia in the 1600s and 1700s, but there wasn't much of a population in places such as Pensacola for centuries.

Over the years since, there have been periods when the area has temporarily grown citrus. As in the rest of Florida, there's always been potted, dooryard or privately grown citrus that would be killed from time to time by the cold weather and replanted.

Marianna in Jackson County, for a short time, was known as the "Satsuma Capital of the World," holding the Marianna Satsuma Orange Festival in the 1920s. The orange festival featured the crowning of a Satsuma Queen, dance performances by local kids, parades and other celebrations. Until all three thousand acres of the Jackson County trees were killed by a hard freeze, it was a major industry for the area, even if it was only between 1900 and 1935.

The Satsuma is an easy-peeling type of Mandarin orange that's very cold-hardy and used more as a fresh fruit product than a juicing one. The few seeds they produce inside the fruit puts them in the category of seedless. It's a sweet-tasting orange (not tart like a standard Tangerine) of medium to large size and has a fantastic aroma as you peel it.

From 2000 to 2018, the southern United States hasn't had much in the way of hard freezes, and a run of warm weather tends to get people growing in places that they weren't before. Dr. Michael Rogers, president

Marianna Satsuma Orange Festival. M.L. Dekle entry in the Satsuma Festival parade. Late 1920s. *Florida Photographic Collection, State Archives of Florida, Florida Memory.*

of University of Florida's Citrus Research and Education Center, said that they've even recently met with commercial growers in Georgia who wanted to know more about the challenges facing citrus growers and how to combat them.

Growers here are encouraged to aim for earlier crops, less for juicing like the Valencia and more for fresh fruit varieties such as Navels and Owari Satsumas, which are the most popular in more northern places such as the Panhandle.

In the 2010s, and even as early as the 2000s, there was some experimentation growing Satsumas in the Panhandle on a commercial basis. Back in the 2000s, a cattleman named Mack Glass, whose family had lived and worked as farmers or ranchers in the area, started trying to bring Satsumas back. Since then, other growers have picked up the gauntlet first thrown down by Glass in '05. Jackson and Gadsden County growers seem to be leading the way in the Panhandle area in the 2010s.

Dooryard trees can be important as well—their presence can be a signal to commercial growers and farmers that growing a crop is viable. In 2008, an organization called Yes We Can Pensacola was begun by asking community members to donate their unwanted fruit, which they would distribute to the needy. One tree can produce far more than a family could ever eat. Reportedly, the group picked 2,500 pounds in the first year, 5,000 the next and 15,000 the third year. Fruit went to several different charity groups, with most going to Manna Food Pantries, and it's also given to other organizations such as Appetite for Life and FavorHouse of Northwest Florida, a center and shelter for victims of domestic violence.

On the commercial side, as of 2016, according to a *Citrus Industry News* article, Callie Walker, chief of the FDACS Bureau of Pest Eradication and Control, said that there's a total of about three hundred acres of citrus growing in the Panhandle, with a maximum of twenty-five acres in one place. That's three hundred acres spread over more than twenty counties, which isn't enough for any of the counties in this area to be included in Florida Department of Agriculture's Citrus Statistics Report. For the orange tourist today, there really aren't any places that we know of to experience U-Pick orange groves or orange history.

Quite a few of the growers in the Panhandle are non-commercial growers with yard trees. As it's difficult to eat all the fruit from the trees in a given season, many growers turn to giving away to neighbors as gifts, donation to charity or by turning their crop into preserves, such as marmalade.

Satsuma Bourbon Marmalade

2 pounds Satsuma
3 cups water
4½ cups sugar
juice of 2 Meyer Lemons
1 teaspoon ground cardamom
½ teaspoon ginger
1–2 tablespoons brown liquor (bourbon, rum or brandy)

Peel and segment the Satsumas, removing the white pith and veiny stuff around them as much as possible. Julienne the peels after you've removed all the pith. Set the peel aside. Chop the orange segments using the pulse button to shred, but don't go wild and turn it into mush.

Bring the segments, peels and 3 cups of water to a boil on stovetop and then reduce to a gentle simmer for 30 minutes or longer.

Add sugar and lemon juice, cooking over low heat, and stir continuously until the sugar has dissolved. Add the cardamom and ginger. Then turn up the heat, bring to a boil and keep at a rolling boil for 20 to 30 minutes or until the setting point is reached. Start testing for setting when a candy thermometer reaches about 220 degrees.

Slowly stir the bourbon into the marmalade, blending it into the mixture as equally as possible. Put the marmalade in warm, sterilized Mason jars, with ¼-inch headspace. Process the jars in a boiling water bath for 5 minutes and then seal. Store in a cool, dark place and refrigerate after opening.

CENTRAL AND NORTH CENTRAL

Where Orange Was King

I n the 1850s, a little less than twenty years after the big-impact freeze of 1835, there were a number of growers who began their enterprises in Central Florida.

Oranges were already firmly a part of Central Florida's landscape before the Civil War, but after the war ended, and everyone seemed to catch orange fever, the groves multiplied exponentially.

As with the rest of the state, Central Florida was hit hard by the 1894–95 and '99 freezes, but production in Central Florida even before that had been higher and of better quality than it ever had been in the northern parts of the state, the major drawback in Central Florida being transportation of both supplies in and oranges out to be sold.

With the expansion of the railway in the late 1800s and early 1900s, and the land boom of the 1910s and early 1920s, the railways solved many of the transport issues, so while Northeast Florida largely gave up on the prospect of oranges, Central Florida, seen as better land for citrus anyway, became the seat of oranges for the state for decades afterward.

THE NORTHERN EDGE

The northernmost of the high-producing Central Florida counties, Alachua, grew the most oranges in the state during the 1889–90 season, with a staggering-for-the-time 817,767 boxes, bursting with groves all

Early citrus packinghouses were often at the docks for ease of transport onto steamboats. St. Johns River at Palatka, 1890s. *Detroit Publishing Company Collection, Library of Congress.*

Railway lines and the citrus industry were vitally connected, both for tourism and transport. Postcard, 1910. *Author's collection.*

around Melrose, Gainesville and Hawthorne. In the 1880s, Gainesville was described as "an island in the midst of orange groves," with the industry taking over everything from dooryards to vacant lots. Before the 1894–95 freeze, the belt around Micanopy was the largest orange producing area in the state.

Although Alachua would never again be the leader of orange production in the state after the 1894–95 freezes, it did rebuild its groves, and it was still enough of a factor to be part of Citrus Mutual's post-freeze surveys for decades afterward. As far north as Alachua is, it's not surprising that with the cold decade of 1895–1906 and a hard freeze in 1917 that brought the temperature to chilly seventeen degrees in Gainesville and a daunting sixteen degrees during a freeze in 1934, it wasn't considered a major industry, even in the 1930s. In an Alachua County promotional pamphlet, circa 1934, citrus is notably absent from the agricultural section, which touted everything from dairy farming to hogs, potatoes, eggplants, watermelons, tobacco and even more obscure items such as tung oil nuts.

By 1989 for certain, there were so few groves left that Alachua was no longer included in the county-by-county freeze damage survey for the state. The county is also no longer included in the industry assessment of citrus production from the Florida Department of Agriculture today.

If you've read Marjorie Kinnan Rawlings's *Cross Creek*, she frequently mentions the groves she bought in 1927, located in the southeastern corner of Alachua, about twenty miles southeast of the Gainesville and twenty-four miles north of Ocala in Marion County. The location, though geographically limited and prone to occasional flooding, is protected somewhat from extreme temperature shifts because it's between Orange and Lochloosa Lakes and the waters create a favorable microclimate. At the Marjorie Kinnan Rawlings Historic State Park, where her home and grounds have been preserved, you can still see a few orange trees there today, although most were killed off in the 1980s. You might also stop in at Cross Creek Groves nearby, a wonderful place to see old Florida.

Another far north Central Florida county that, like Alachua, got dropped for the county-by-county freeze damage by at least 1989 was Putnam County. The county contained the city of Palatka, once dubbed the "Home of the Orange" and "Gem City of the St. Johns." Palatka in the 1850s was reportedly rife with oranges and booming by the early 1890s. But in promotional material for Putnam and Palatka, by the 1960s, citrus crops aren't noted—instead, potatoes and cabbages are the leading produce, with nary a mention of oranges as an agricultural crop.

But Putnam isn't completely bereft of oranges even today. Although Putnam is one of the lowest producers of oranges in the state (it was lumped in with Citra County in a Florida Department of Agriculture report for 2015–16 with a total of just twenty-three thousand boxes of citrus between them), like a lot of counties that don't have a big industry impact, there are small groves and private sellers to be found if you're willing to search for them. As of 2016 and early 2017, probably one of the most northern groves is San Mateo's Cecil Nelson Citrus in Putnam. African American owners Nelson and his wife have been growing citrus, including oranges, on their land for about thirty years. They bought the ten acres and from a frustrated citrus farmer, who sold it to them after a bad freeze in the late 1980s. The seventy-three-year-old owner has had real estate interest in the property, and although he loves working the land, retirement is a possibility. In a *Northeast Florida Edible* article, he was quoted as saying that he's "an old guy, but I don't sit around watching TV," and although he has help during harvest, he's out daily tending to his grove. If he's still around and growing citrus by the time you read this, he might be found at the Beaches Green Market in Jacksonville Beach or at the Union Street Farmers' Market in Gainesville during the harvest season, bewitching passersby with fragrant slices of citrus samples.

CITRA PIONEERS AND PINEAPPLE ORANGES

One of the early serious commercial growers in Marion County was a man named John A. Harris (later dubbed the "Orange King of Florida"), who began planting just after the Civil War around 1870. He noted the presence of wild oranges in the hammocks of Florida when he came to the state, something he attributed to the Native American population, saying, "All the wild orange groves of any size in Florida are always found signs of Indian habitation—Indian mounds, where they buried their dead, arrow heads, pottery."

These "wild" groves were both an enticement and a trial to these pioneers of the industry. In a paper for the Florida Horticulture Society, A.S. Kells described those early groves:

> *The cultivation of these dense wild orange groves was very difficult. Some of the wild orange trees were six to eight inches in diameter; and they grew so thick that it was impossible to walk through without first cutting a path. Many had to be cut down; others were dug up, and transplanted as new*

land could be prepared. Later on some were sold to new comers. These wild groves were not in straight lines, as the orange groves of today, but were here and there in their original stand. The wild trees were cut off and budded, and produced fruit in two years from the bud.

Kells reported that orange growers were coming back from the Big Freeze of 1894–95, saying that "with the same perseverance and energy which characterized their first attacks on the wild groves, the Citra growers at once pruned back and rebudded their trees, and the present thrifty groves are the result."

Citra's largest claim to fame, the Pineapple Orange, was developed just prior to the big 1894–95 freeze, and it spread throughout the state. J.B. Owens owned nine sweet orange trees grown from seed, just four and a half miles from Citra. When the fruit was ripe, Owens thought one of the trees had an aroma a bit like pineapple, and so he named it the Pineapple Orange. Contrary to the name, it doesn't taste anything like a pineapple. Owens sold buds from all his trees to P.P. Bishop, and Bishop developed the orange further and grafted it onto sour.

Some concerns near Citra, such as Crosby-Wartman Groves, began specializing in Pineapple Oranges by the 1910s, marketing them to New York, Philadelphia, Chicago and even internationally in the next few decades. Although Pineapple Oranges tend not to be cold-hardy, the

Left: Citrus label for Mocking Bird, one of the companies in Citra and Florida's State Bird. *Brenda Eubanks Burnette personal collection.*

Opposite: Pineapple Orange. U.S. Department of Agriculture Pomological Watercolor Collection, Rare and Special Collections, National Agricultural Library, Beltsville, MD, 20705.

No. 53431
Pineapple.
C. S. Pomeroy.
Chas. J. King Jr.
Wildwood.
Sumpter Co., Fla.

E. J. Schutt
March 21 – 1911
April 3 – 1911

Crosby-Wartman Groves survived the freezes of 1917 and 1934 and the little temperature drops in between with the then-innovative use of grove heaters. This wasn't their only innovation, as they were one of the first to adopt the use of refrigerated railway cars to transport and preserve citrus.

The Crosby-Wartman Groves produced until the death of both owners in the 1940s, when it was divided by heirs. In 1973, part of the grove was sold off to a partnership of Buddy McKay, Jim Williams, Elton Clemmons and H.L. Clemmons Jr. This partnership bought up more of the land in 1978. They fought the 1980s freezes as best they could, but by the freeze of 1985, the weakened trees had not survived and the partnership gave the land over to other uses.

FIGHTING THE FREEZES OF THE TWENTIETH CENTURY IN McINTOSH

There were, of course, lots of freezes to fight in the twentieth century, before the terrible cold decade of the 1980s, pushing what Florida growers perceived as the "frostline" more and more south. For a detailed account of the freezes, *A History of Florida Citrus Freezes* by citrus luminary John Attaway will take you through every major freeze to the 1990s. It's an amazing and detailed resource used throughout this book.

McIntosh, along Orange Lake in the southern region of Marion County, held on until the cataclysmic freezes of the 1980s. Some of the most prominent groves were those of O.D. Buddy Huff's, which were the first you could see on the 441 drive from Gainesville.

O.D. Buddy's widow, Ollie, in a 2006 *Ocala Star Banner* story, said that she considered the property "up on the hill" an important part of her and her husband's history. "It was where O.D. proposed. It's where we had our Orange Shop and McIntosh is really where we lived for 32 years.…Why, I worked hard at that Orange Shop, the hardest I ever worked! I used to say that was the main reason that O.D. kept me around, because I made some good money there."

Ollie related that fighting freezes was a family affair, with her husband in constant contact with the Frost Warning Service, their daughter checking thermometers placed strategically throughout the grove and their son rounding up the workers to light and fill the twenty-one thousand heaters.

The grove's manager, Dick Whittington, said that over a period of some thirty years, there were only two seasons in which they did not fire or use heaters in the grove. Buddy stayed on top of his groves, reportedly never

A card advertising temperature alarms from sometime in the first half of the 1900s. *Glen St. Mary Nursery Collection.*

more than two miles away at any given time, and judiciously pruning back the dead growth whenever the freeze won a bit of his trees.

Of the 1980s freezes, Whittington was quoted as saying, "Buddy died July 12, 1984. He saw the damage from the December 1983 freeze, but I don't think he realized that every tree was killed to the ground. Knowing Buddy he would have pushed out the stumps and planted again."

The Huff family got out of the business, selling the heaters and then leasing remaining grove land (which was converted into pasture), a good decision considering that they would have had to start all over again—the terrible 1985 and '89 freezes were still to come.

MARION COUNTY TODAY AND THE ORANGE SHOP IN CITRA

Nearly every scrap of land along every country road around Ocala in Marion County had been overtaken by oranges in 1875, but a century later, with a few big freezes and all the small ones in between, oranges were no longer a big industry around the city, with horse farms and other concerns buying up the land. Although the southern portions of Marion County have soldiered on, Ocala just wasn't a substantial part of the citrus game any longer by the late 1970s.

While there were small concerns and growers in Marion County after the 1980s, the majority of huge commercial groves are gone. A Florida Department of Agriculture report still lists Marion as producer as of the 2015–16 season, with 163,000 boxes, categorized in the lowest tier of production for the state. But while the production might be lower, you're more likely to find "eating oranges" rather than juicing oranges, which make up the majority of oranges grown and produced in most recent years.

Juice a Hamlin or a Valencia, and it stays sweet in the glass, but juice an eating orange, like an Ambersweet or the new Sugar Belle, and it quickly goes flat or develops bitter, sour notes. Eating oranges, because of their more volatile chemistry, are far more fragrant and flavorful than a juicing orange, but they don't hold their flavor profile for long once exposed to oxygen, which is why they are for eating and not for juicing.

Today, about twenty-five miles south of Ocala, in Weirsdale, you can find a U-Pick family-run grove called Hilltop Groves, which sells Navel oranges, Ruby Red grapefruit, Fall tangerines and Ambersweets, an orange/tangelo mix, as well as sometimes Honeybells. Its season generally starts in late October, running through whenever it runs out, which can be anytime in late March to early May.

You'll also want to visit the simply named Orange Shop in Citra. Little fruit shipping gift shops like these keep fresh fruit alive as a tradition in the state.

There's a hidden advantage to the lower temperatures of places like Citra, as opposed to the more southerly portions of the state. Most modern Florida oranges end up inside a bottle as Florida orange juice, but before the advent of orange juice around World War II, people wanted beautiful "eating oranges," whole as they were on the tree.

Today, the mid- to late-harvested Valencia orange is the orange of choice, as it's best for juicing, but during the height of orange tourism and orange box gifts, it was the Navel orange that was the choice. At the Orange Shop, they still sell Navels that are grown in Marion County. A Navel orange, if you've never seen one, is a seedless orange that has a depression like a navel, containing an undeveloped tiny secondary fruit.

A Navel does best when temperatures drop low enough to "finish" the fruit—turn them more orange and flavorful, but not so low that they're damaged. Marion County's Navel oranges are arguably some of the best in the state because temperatures get low enough and the soil quality is suited to the fruit.

While you can find fruit shippers in Florida across the Internet, the Orange Shop has an actual storefront open to the public. It opened for business in 1936, catering to the tourists along Highway 301 who wanted to bring back a taste of Florida to their northern homes. The shop's owners, Pete and Cindy Spyke, are third-generation citrus growers, and other members of their family still run their other enterprise down south in Davie Florida, Spyke's Grove, which is today more of a nursery enterprise and a place fruit moves through to order. The Orange Shop, though, does have its own groves, and the supply of fruit comes from what it grows, supplemented with local oranges from Marion, as well as oranges from the celebrated Indian River area. The Spyke family also has groves near Fort Pierce, in St. Lucie County, on the rich soil along Ten Mile Creek, where they grow specialty and spring varieties for the shop: Honeybells, Temples and Tangerines.

THE PARSON BROWN: A RARE VINTAGE FIND FROM SUMTER COUNTY

Parson Brown. U.S. Department of Agriculture Pomological Watercolor Collection, Rare and Special Collections, National Agricultural Library, Beltsville, MD, 20705.

If you're wanting an orange that's utterly vintage and utterly Central Florida, look no further than the Parson Brown orange, although it may take you a while to find one.

The Parson Brown gets its quirky name from the man who first grew them in his yard near Webster (located in modern-day Sumter County) around 1856. Reverend N.L. Parson wasn't a commercial grower, but he sold the propagation rights in the 1870s to J.L. Carney, who named it Parson Brown and budded the first commercial versions of the fruit on to sour oranges, probably on Lake Weir's Carney Island in Marion County.

It's a decidedly Florida orange because it never caught on in California. If you're looking to eat a seedless orange, the Parson is not for you; however, it's reportedly excellent for fresh-squeezed orange juice at home and fun to eat, if you don't mind the seeds. The skin is thick, finely pebbled and leans more toward yellow than orange. It was a very popular cultivar through the 1920s and still a major variety through the late 1960s. Since the majority of today's commercial oranges are of the late variety (like the Valencia), it's not convenient for large-scale growers to keep because they have the most access to labor in the late season. It can still be found today in Florida nurseries as seedlings, and is sometimes sold as a specialty fruit by online retailers and at U-Pick Farms, but is vanishingly rare.

HOWEY-IN-THE-HILLS AND THE FLORIDA LAND BOOM

William John Howey, born in Odin, Illinois, in 1875, became one of the most important figures in citrus from about 1910 through the 1930s.

Howey was an entrepreneur to his core, first selling insurance for several different companies and then helping to develop land and towns for the railway in Oklahoma, later manufacturing and designing cars in Missouri and finally developing and selling pineapple land in Mexico. These jobs prepared him for his enterprise in Florida.

Insurance sales in the 1890s was not the staid job it might be seen as today. Large-scale insurance operations began to crop up everywhere, and since they were as of yet largely unregulated, scandal naturally followed. Some companies ran Ponzi-like schemes, luring as many insurers in as they could at lower rates and only paying out claims as long as new sales were strong—or going bust with the first expensive claim. Others used the lack of regulation to form monopolies and ask for outrageous premiums. For a born salesman such as Howey, insurance was the perfect job—unregulated enough that there weren't extra expenses or restrictions but just familiar enough to the public as a product to be easily sold and marketed.

After his insurance gigs, Howey helped Oklahoma develop land and settlements with the backing of a railway company. This experience, more than any other, probably taught him the crucial ingredients needed for a successful town, along with how to attract the people and needed services.

When he opened Howey Automobile Company in Kansas City in 1903, he ended up using a completely different skill set, as he had seven Howey cars manufactured, but he lasted only two years in this enterprise, switching back to land development—this time with an added, delicious twist: pineapples. Mexico pineapple land had everything he could want to sell to American investors (and many of the elements he would later use in his sales on orange lands in Florida): a moneymaking agricultural product, a touch of the exotic, plenty of land to develop and not a lot of regulation in his way. But the revolution in 1907 put a kibosh on his plans. So Howey turned his development and salesmanship talents to Florida and oranges in 1908, starting with land near Winter Haven and present-day Dundee. While there, he met Dr. Frederick W. Inman, who introduced him to the idea of budding sweet oranges on rough lemon rootstock, a technique that produced salable fruit within six years of planting the rootstock.

Using the railway to promote and get investors into Dundee, he set up a tent city to start with. His efforts caught the attention of two citrus pioneers in Lake County, attorney Harry Duncan and Sheriff Balton A. Cassady, who asked him to look over and develop land in their county. Liking the area near a chain of lakes adjacent to Little Lake Harris, by 1920 Howey had bought up sixty thousand acres.

By the 1910s, he'd upgraded to a civilized hotel for prospective investors to stay in, selling both the Dundee land in Polk County and his new pieces of land in Lake County, near Lake Harris. Although World War I slowed his momentum, at the war's end, he was poised to sell and develop his own town.

The way it worked was this: Howey would sell a piece of his grove to the investor and then would manage the groves for the investor as part of the contract. The investor would be responsible for paying expenses (making Howey's management enterprise a profit along the way) that would be taken out of the profit that the groves made, and Howey sweetened the deal further—if the grove didn't return the investment by the eleventh year, his company would repurchase the grove for a price equal to the land, the planting and maintenance plus 6 percent interest.

Howey's gimmicks, like an automobile caravan from Chicago to Florida in 1920, got him the press he needed to sell, along with offices everywhere he could put them, from all the resort cities of Florida, to as many northern and midwestern cities as he could manage. By 1925, he had named his enterprise near Lake Harris, which was now a town, Howey-in-the-Hills, and he'd added a golf course.

Howey's development rode the wave of the Florida Land Boom, but even when the boom went bust in 1926, although his sales continued to drop, he had several more years of success. Despite a further sales dip with the Great Depression in 1929, he continued to sell shares at a decent rate through 1930, maintaining his operation through fruit sales rather than land sales.

In 1927, for a sum of $250,000, Howey's mansion was completed. That same year, he opened a juice bottling plant, the better to make profits from

Foyer of the Howey House. *By Shanejayhayes, Wikimedia Commons.*

unsalable ugly fruit, misshapen or slightly damaged on the outside but perfectly delicious inside.

Other orange growers followed his model of shares in citrus land, but he wasn't the first to do so. As far back as the 1870s, others, such as the Florida Orange Grove Company and J.O. Matthews, sold shares of citrus land in Marion County near Orange Lake, and they even included an option of land for investors to build cottages, offering to procure lumber to build them, another way for the company to line its pockets. But Howey's success and the sheer number of offices he opened all over the country to sell and develop the town he founded certainly made an indelible impression on the citrus industry.

Howey's name and the sales of his groves have recently come up in news because of a legal precedent set by the Supreme Court when the SEC sued his concern for selling "unregistered and nonexempt" securities in the 1940s. While what Howey had been doing hadn't been strictly illegal at the time and in a rather gray area of the law, this ruling better defined what securities were, so the more than seventy-year-old ruling is coming up regarding crypto currencies, as the "Howey Test" determines what a security is. From a recent *Forbes* article on the subject:

> [A]*lthough citrus and crypto couldn't be more different asset classes, one tangible, the other virtual, there are eerie parallels to then and now. Howey's investment creativity took place against the backdrop of the industrial revolution, the invention of the automobile and the creation of the transcontinental railroad. Today's ICO innovations are taking place against the backdrop of the data revolution and the evolution of the internet through blockchain technology.*

The Howey Test essentially determines that an investment contract is an investment of money with the expectation of profits, entirely from the efforts of others. The Supreme Court said that Howey's company offered "something different from a farm or orchard coupled with management services." Instead, it was "an opportunity to contribute money and to share in the profits of a large citrus fruit enterprise managed and partly owned by respondents." Gold, for example, is not a security because the value of the investment depends on market forces rather than a specific entity. But something like the stock of a company, where the value is largely dependent on the actions of a company, is a security. The ruling from the Supreme Court was broad enough that it has stood the test of time for more than seven decades.

Given Howey's enthusiasm for Florida's development, the door to politics opened easily to him, first as the mayor of the town he founded and later with two runs for governor in 1928 and 1932.

At the time of his first run for governor, the state of Florida was wholly Democrat. This was because even decades after the Civil War, the Republicans were seen as the party of racial tolerance—the party of Lincoln and Grant. They aren't seen that way today, partly because of the efforts of William Howey and other men like him. He helped foster the "lily white" Republican movement in Florida, built on a foundation of white supremacy and limiting the political and monetary power growing within the black and mixed-race communities. The movement began in Texas but spread throughout the South. Howey may or may not have agreed with the racist tenets of the lily white movement, but probably he did know that it was the only realistic way to get the Republican Party started in the state. He considered the one-party system then in place intrinsically corrupt. Like many politicians, he was not above saying what he thought his base wanted to hear. Howey came out as staunchly for the enforcement of the Volstead Act, while secretly keeping a liquor vault in his mansion.

The arguments against Howey as a gubernatorial candidate are surprisingly familiar: his competitors said that he wasn't running to win, but that he just wanted publicity. With the publicity he would benefit and be able to promote and sell more land.

While Howey didn't win in 1928, he accomplished the one thing that the Republicans had been aiming at: a two-party system in Florida. Before Howey's run, Florida basically had a one-party system, and per the rules, it was only allowed to have primary elections for another party in the event that the party captured at least 30 percent of the vote in a statewide race. Since Howey had gotten 39 percent of the vote, the Republicans now had the right to organize and run as a true party in the state.

Howey became a leader in the party, running again for governor in 1932. It was a bit harder to market himself as a business success this time because Howey-in-the-Hills was in major debt, and Democratic newspapers criticized Howey for running a business that was losing money. In the depths of the Great Depression, running on a prosperity platform could not and did not work, and Howey lost again.

Howey died just five years later in 1938, leaving a quite a legacy: a founded town, a Florida party built and forward-thinking ideas that would become the basis for the age of orange juice after World War II.

In 2015, the residents of Howey-in-the-Hills celebrated the ninetieth year since its incorporation with a birthday cake decorated with a picture of the town's water tower. Present at the celebration were two of Howey's granddaughters, and although neither had met William John Howey, they'd grown up on stories of his exploits, with one granddaughter quoted in an *Orlando Sentinel* article as saying, "Our grandmother said he had a silver tongue." As of 2017, real estate developer Clayton Cowherd and his brother, Brad, bought the Howey family mansion and restored the place. Today, it's being used as an events venue, favored for weddings.

LAKE COUNTY TODAY AND ORANGE ATTRACTIONS TO VISIT

Lake County for the 2015–16 season had a respectable 1,606,000 boxes, according to the Department of Agriculture. That's certainly nowhere near what its production was during the height of orange growing in the 1970s, and it's far behind the top three counties of Hendry, DeSoto and Polk, which averaged about 13 million boxes for the 2015–16 season. As of 2015, about ten thousand acres were devoted to citrus in Lake County. The neighboring Orange

County citrus growers sold off many of their groves in the 1960s once real estate prices skyrocketed, but the bulk of Lake County held on until the freezes of the 1980s. But development and land value have caught up with the county, and today, growers in Lake County must resist the enormous profit of selling their land, even in the face of citrus greening, canker and black spot. Vestiges of orange culture for the tourists remain in the county in the form of U-Pick farms, citrus shops and Clermont's Citrus Tower.

The Citrus Tower of Clermont, built in 1956, attracted tourists wanting a view of the surrounding groves from a lofty height of twenty-two stories. These days, you can see the surrounding development, but there's not much to view as far as oranges are concerned. It has great memorabilia, maps and

The hills of Clermont, which would have been visible from the Clermont Citrus Tower, sadly gone after the 1986 freeze. From the 1940s. *Brenda Eubanks Burnette personal collection.*

photos of what the view used to look like, as well as a tourist gift shop selling Citrus Tower–branded items. For a slice of old Florida orange culture, it's not a bad attraction to visit. The price to ride up to the top is six dollars for adults and four dollars for kids.

To find oranges in a natural setting in Lake County, head to Sabal Bluff Preserve in Leesburg. It's mostly a nature preserve and a park, but there are still a few citrus trees growing wild there, mainly around the Lake Griffin trail, which provides a microclimate warm enough to protect the citrus.

In Umatilla, you can find a piece of vintage Florida orange history in front of Sunsational Citrus. It's known as the "Big Orange," and it didn't begin its life in Lake County. First displayed in Polk County as part of orange tourism, it was bought by Tommy Sanders as a promotional tool for his Lake County business, Orange Car, in 1971. He found it sitting in a field off Highway 27 near Lakeland and bought it for just $1,500. Eventually, the giant orange was moved, decaying under vines and mold in the woods off Highway 441 for a good thirty years, until it was bought in 2015 by the owners of Sunsational Citrus. They had it hauled to their shop, restoring it with forty hours of sandblasting, three coats of primer and nine gallons of acrylic orange paint, as well as a new wooden floor.

Inside their shop they have displays of vintage citrus juicers and a few framed articles and pictures on citrus history, as well as a plaque honoring Nick Faryna, the former patriarch of the clan who died in 2014. Faryna started his business in 1967 with Sharon, his wife, working at his side. They began by managing the family's 20 acres of citrus, eventually handling as much as 3,500 acres. Nick went to school, getting a degree in fruit crop production in 1973 from UF. When a major freeze hit in 1977, he wasn't scared away, but instead started experimenting with microsprinklers to save groves from freezes. By the '89 freeze, most of the Central Florida growers had adopted the technique. This, along with work on targeted herbicide application and work with IFAS and the USDA on rootstock and scion trials, earned him a place in the Citrus Hall of Fame. He moved on to open a packinghouse and belonged to myriad growers associations and advisory committees.

Today, his family keeps citrus alive in Lake County with their country store, Sunsational Citrus. Nick and Sharon's daughter, Lauren Sutton, helps to manage their off-site groves, as well as the shop. Lauren, with her mother and father's family line, is the fourth generation to be involved in Florida's orange industry. Sunsational sells orange ice cream, citrus products, honey, fruit wines, orange kitsch, fresh juice and oranges, when they're available.

THE SECRET GROVE OF OSCEOLA COUNTY

Deep in Osceola County, early settlers knew that there lay hidden a grove unusual for the Indians, one the white man did not find until fifty years after the natives had left the area—and then only by accident.

The area around Kissimmee hadn't yet been fully drained, the waterlogged land being dotted with little islands of earth in the thick jungle-like undergrowth. The Seminoles would emerge loaded down with oranges, but the white settlers never could get the location of their hidden grove, not through persuasion and certainly not via white-led scouting parties, who searched in vain.

A hunter, said to be a Mr. I.E. Moseley, out running his dogs to flush deer, stumbled on the secret grove on a series of small hammocks or islands in the swampland in the late 1800s or early 1900s. What made the grove unusual was the nature of the oranges—they were sweet, not sour or bitter.

This sweet grove might have been originally grown from an exception to the rule of the seed being unlike the parent. Rarely will an orange be true to seed, and when it is, its children are likely to be so as well. These rarities are both prized and cursed—because they can't easily be cross-bred—but are valued because what's grown will be consistent. Citrus growers can and do nurture and propagate a tree like this with good characteristics.

It's also likely the Seminoles situated the grove in a microclimate perfect for the oranges grown there, as being surrounded by water can often moderate the temperature. The spot where the grove is said to have been located was in swamplands about ten miles from Kissimmee (north or south isn't indicated), by the junction of three creeks running at the time: Davenport, Reedy and Bennett. Development has changed the landscape, and we do not know where the grove was. As was the case with other groves, artifacts such as broken pottery and an Indian mound were found near to the site. Reportedly, as of the 1930s, the area remained swampy, and good hunting land besides.

KISSIMMEE, A CROSSROADS

Production of citrus, while part of the scene in Osceola County historically, has never been wildly high, although around the 1930s, Osceola Fruit Distributors was the largest employer in the county. Other enterprises, such as raising cattle, have been more of a cultural touchstone for residents than citrus farming. Still, Kissimmee's strategic location, as a place where many railroads crossed early in the 1900s, and then later as a place where highways crossed as well, made it a prime location for citrus packing or juicing with fruit from the surrounding areas.

OSCEOLA COUNTY TODAY

While Osceola did a bit more in citrus than Lake County as of 2016–17, and the numbers from both counties can fluctuate, their output in the past decade is comparable. In square miles, the county is about four hundred square miles bigger than Lake County. Oseola averaged about 1,314,000 boxes of oranges for the 2015–16 season and the 2016–17 season, according to the USDA's Florida Citrus statistics.

Osceola County has two orange attractions of note: Florida Orange World, where you can buy in-season fresh oranges, and the Pioneer Village, which generally does not have fresh oranges but does have lots of interesting early settler homes, pulled from various areas of the county; replica Indian dwellings, or chickees; and orange-related artifacts in the restored Camden packinghouse.

Narcoossee in Osceola County had a bit of a "British Invasion" in the 1880s, when wealthy investors from England settled there. The English family of note, whose complex has been moved to the Pioneer Village along with their fruit packinghouse, was the Cadman clan, who grew and packed citrus in the area until the big freeze in 1894–95. The packinghouse was moved to Pioneer Village in Kissimmee in 2005 as part of an outdoor exhibition on pioneer life, which you can see today. Once the freeze hit, the good majority of British growers moved on, either growing more south or going elsewhere and getting into another enterprise entirely, but you can see this glimpse into life back then and how they packed oranges, including an early orange sorter, operated by pedaling and a pulley. The custom was to wrap each orange in paper coated with beeswax and linseed oil, which, according to the Pioneer Village website, was an invention claimed by the Cadmans.

THE SANFORD EXPERIMENT

Henry Shelton Sanford didn't live his life in his gardens and groves, tending to his plants. He was a man of the world, and he traveled through it with a regularity that probably stunted the profit he might have gotten from horticulture back in Florida.

Born in 1823 in Connecticut, he dropped out of college in 1841 after an asthmatic condition caused his eyesight to deteriorate. Instead, he traveled Europe, learning languages and studying European culture. By 1847, he'd begun his lifelong career as a diplomat, serving as an attaché and secretary of the American Legation at St. Petersburg. Serving in various diplomatic posts, he was eventually given the post of United States minister to Belgium by President Abraham Lincoln in 1861. During the Civil War, he served as more than a mere diplomat in Europe, and his true job was in intelligence, gathering information on the South as it attempted to get support from

Henry Shelton Sanford. *Library of Congress, Prints and Photographs Division.*

Europe. Using private detectives and his own network, he sent information back to the Union, sabotaging Confederate efforts such as shipbuilding and supply smuggling.

General Henry Shelton Sanford founded the city named for himself, buying Florida land in 1868, just a few years after the Civil War. Finding that labor in Florida was a problem, Sanford imported Swedes in the 1870s and '80s as indentured servants, agreeing to pay their passage to the United States after one year of labor. As a lifelong politician, diplomat and explorer, he used his international connections to procure botanical samples from all over the world, establishing the Belair Grove, where these samples were grown and agriculturalists measured their viability in the Florida climate. Many of the samples came from Africa because of his connections with the Congo. He was named acting delegate of the American Geographical Society to a conference called by King Leopold II of Belgium in 1876. The conference was intended to "civilize" equatorial Africa or, at the very least, introduce the cultures there to education and concepts from the Western world. His efforts led to the formation of the independent state of the Congo, and he worked over his lifetime to get the United States to invest money there.

At Belair, Sanford grew everything from subtropical ornamentals to olives, coffee and citrus of all kinds. But it was the oranges that had the most variety, with more than one hundred different types grown on site, imported from various parts of the world. Buds from trees grown here were sold at little to no cost, so Sanford's legacy, although it lacks in oranges today, is that the land and city helped to spread many different types of oranges throughout the state prior to the Big Freeze of 1894–95. For a time in the 1880s, Sanford, Florida, seemed destined to become a center of citrus and "a gateway to Southern Florida."

We have the perspective of history to call 1894–95 the Big Freeze, but in a pamphlet out in 1889 entitled *Some Account of Belair, also of the City of Sanford Florida with a Brief Sketch of Their Founder*, the unnamed author wrote of the "Big Freeze" of 1886 with no idea of what was to come. Still, the freezes of the 1880s and particularly 1886 discouraged Sanford somewhat. Before the freeze of 1886, he'd been devoted to agricultural experimentation, testing various methods to see what would grow and how, with one hundred varieties of citrus on the land, some decades before the Lake Alfred experimental station began in 1917. In fact, he'd unsuccessfully petitioned Washington in 1884 to use one hundred acres he offered up as a donation for experiments of its own. The promotional pamphlet of 1889 reads like an argument for government backing of the experiments.

Before the real Big Freeze of 1894–95, Sanford, Florida, was a powerhouse of orange shipping, with an estimated seventeen thousand boxes to go out from the city in 1889, but once the tree-killing freezes hit, farmers decided to try something new—namely celery. Henry Sanford died in 1891, so he never saw the devastation of the freezes that collapsed the orange industry in Sanford. By the 1910s, celery had replaced citrus as the main crop of Sanford, earning it the nickname of "Celery City" through the 1970s.

THE GOOD DOCTOR FOSTER AND OVIEDO'S FIGHT WITH THE PLANT RAILROAD

Oviedo had its share of stalwart pioneers and characters in the 1870s and 1880s, but the standout, Dr. Henry Foster, was an orange grove investor from New York State.

He saved up enough money to begin his own practice but still needed investors, so he installed a board of directors for his own hydrotherapy practice, the Clifton Springs Sanitorium in New York State, which he opened in 1850. By 1867, he had bought out all the stockholders and was the sole owner of his practice.

Deeply religious from a young age, he built a chapel on the grounds of his Sanitorium and believed in the power of prayer alongside the practices of a simple, healthful diet and water treatments. Always charitable, he used his profits to house ill ministers, their families and teachers at little or no cost to them.

His practice wore on him enough that he craved restorative recreation, eventually adopting the practice of a two- or three- month vacation each year. As early as 1867, the good doctor hunted along Florida's St. Johns River. At Palatka, he met a Captain Meredith Brock, an ex-Confederate soldier who extolled the virtues of the hunting and fishing to be found around Lake Jesup, which was near what was to become Oviedo, Florida.

Foster was already a man of wealth by this time, claiming $200,000 worth of real estate on an 1860 census, but he sought a winter home, and on the shores of Lake Charm, he found one. He married late, at fifty-one years old, to the thirty-four-year-old daughter of a patient in 1874, the same year that the Gwynns gifted him (or rather his wife) a plot of land on which he had built a house so snug that it stood until the 1940s, only torn down as the result of hurricane damage.

The reason for the gift had to do with a great favor he had done the Gwynns. Visiting the community, he'd befriended Mr. and Mrs. Gwynn and found Mrs. Gwynn deathly ill. Fearing that she would not last until he came back again, he offered to take her to his Sanitorium for treatment, free of charge. When he brought her back again the next year, restored and healthy, as the Gwynns had no money but plenty of hammock lands, they offered up acreage as a gift of thanks. The doctor refused, but they insisted, and he finally acquiesced by having them deed it to his new wife.

Foster carried religion wherever he went, sometimes with sobering effect, not simply because he was an ardent supporter of the temperance movement but also because the wild men of Oviedo began coming to Sunday service once he appeared. Sometimes his influence had an exuberant effect, as was the case with Mrs. Gwynn, who upon returning from the Sanitorium set on the community with religious zeal, resulting in a reported mass conversion.

Foster wasn't all piety though—he liked to tell the story of the time he shot a gator who had boarded his boat. From his biography:

> *In the winter of '67 in company with other gentlemen, Dr. Foster bought a steam launch and cruised on the St. John River, hunting and fishing. The Doctor was a sure shot with a rifle, a skillful angler and a boon companion. One day a sixteen foot alligator pursued the Doctor who was in a row boat*

with a negro. The 'gator's head was on the boat and his jaws wide open. He was all fight. It was a perilous moment, but a well directed bullet from the Doctor's rifle solved the problem. The Doctor, when telling it, said the negro was positively pale from fright.

He had a strength of personality backed by the idea that what he did was part of God's plan, something that was sometimes frustrated when he had to count on others, as it was in later dealings with other orange growers in Oviedo. Like many entrepreneurs, he checked in to see that others were doing their jobs. He frequently stalked the halls of his Sanitorium at night, ensuring that the patients were cared for; in one instance from his biography:

[Foster] *found the night watchman, whom he was suspecting of negligence, in a bathroom sound asleep, his feet stretched out before him and his head tilted back against the wall. The doctor quietly stole the slippers from the watchman's feet and then, getting a bucket of ice cold water, he dashed it all in the sleeper's face. While the bewildered man was trying to get his whereabouts, and to find his slippers, the Doctor stood laughing and went off without saying a word. The man was never again found napping.*

In Oviedo and the surrounding area, his money and personality made him a man of influence. He became a director of a bank at Sanford and a trustee of Rollins College and built a chapel and parsonage at Lake Charm.

When he went back north each year, Foster served as an evangelist for the appeal of the land, convincing many others to buy and set groves in the area: W.S. Farwell of Chicago bought fifty acres at his urging, building a large house with nine fireplaces because Mrs. Farwell thought Florida too cold in winter; William Deering, a manufacturer of farm machines, also bought land though he never built—his sons preferred Miami. Calvin Whitney, president of A.B. Chase Piano, built his grand winter manor in 1886. The community also attracted a hotel built by O.H. Brewster in 1877.

As of the early '70s, Foster planted groves around the cottage at Lake Charm, as well as at his Gee Hammock land. By the mid-1880s, he had fifty acres of groves, and by 1889, he'd reckoned that the land and plantings had paid for themselves, plus 8 percent interest.

One wrinkle that Foster and other Oviedo grove owners had to deal with was the problem of transportation. They had bearing groves but no simple way to get the oranges to the nexus of sales and gateway to the North: Jacksonville. The line from Jacksonville to Sanford wasn't complete until 1886.

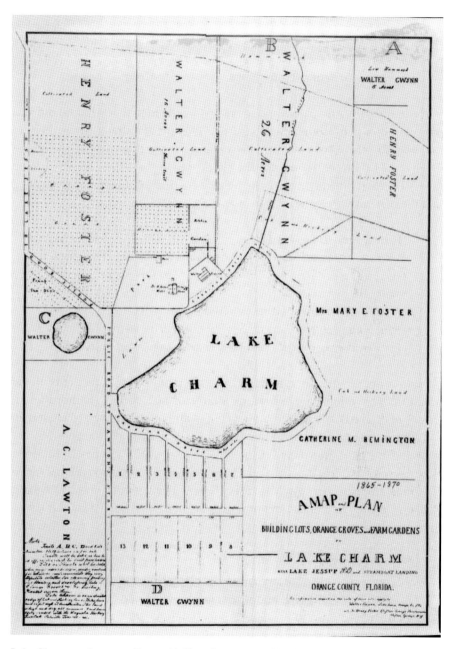

Lake Charm and surroundings, with Foster's groves, and land around the lake the Gwynns had given to his wife, Mary. *Oviedo Historical Society Collection.*

Foster tried to organize stopgap solutions. First, in the early 1880s, he and other moneyed individuals in the community sought to form their own steamboat company. The nearby Lake Jesup connected to a series of lakes that emptied into the St. Johns River, an alternate route to Jacksonville. Lake Jesup had a shallow draft, but one independent steamboat captain by the name of Eugene Bigelow had been sailing it, on a flat-bottomed stern-wheeler called the *Isis* that he'd outfitted nicely with staterooms and a saloon for his passengers. The Lake Jessup Steamboat Company added another stack to the *Isis*, which already had one smokestack, two boilers, two engines and a sturdy iron hull, in December 1881. It's not known if they ever shipped any oranges on board, as in November 1882 the *Isis* ran into a storm on Lake George, capsizing the vessel, rendering it unsalvageable, and killing three crewmen.

In 1888, Foster also formed the Lake Charm Improvement Company, which, while it didn't solve any transportation problems (because Charm didn't connect to anything), was meant to make it more navigable by removing the muck, then used as fertilizer for the surrounding groves, and by installing a drain line from Lake Love (aka Crystal Lake) to keep water levels higher, but the line never did work properly. The company got as far as building a sidewalk around the lake, but things got contentious when the members couldn't agree and the company fell apart.

With the coming of the railway so close to Oviedo in Sanford, Foster wanted to make sure there would be a spur into Oviedo and near Lake Charm, where his groves were, so he paid the Sanford & Indian River Railroad to bring it for $5,000, no small sum for the day.

Since the plan of a steamboat cooperative had failed some five years before, orange growers rejoiced at the coming of the railroad in 1886. But as they were the last on the line of the St. Johns River (connected to them via a lake system), the Plant Railroad System, the parent company to the Sanford and Indian River Railroad, had a monopoly. When it opened the line, it charged five cents per box of oranges to Jacksonville, but in late 1887 or early 1888, it more than doubled its shipping rate to eleven cents per box. The outraged growers complained, but the railroad wouldn't budge. Foster even went to Tallahassee to plead their case and have the railway commission force the line to lower its rates. But the commission did nothing, so Foster and other growers hatched a plan—they'd build their own damn railroad.

The motivated growers put their money together to form the Oviedo, Lake Charm & Lake Jesup Railroad, incorporated on October 26, 1888.

Frederick DeBary, whose steamboat line was being fast overtaken by the railways as the mode of transport for people and goods, offered to haul the oranges out of Lake Jesup if they could get them to Solary's Wharf by rail. DeBary, who mainly lived in Volusia County, still bought forty shares of the new rail company, and Foster bought twenty, each share being fifty dollars. Once formed, the company moved with celerity, and it may have already had a surveyor out even before it incorporated.

Getting money out of the growers proved difficult, and when they bought the rails DeBary ended up holding a mortgage on them for $1,500. But by July 1889, the concern had bought land for the right-of-way and a pole cart. There were meant to have been two lines, one from Lake Charm to Solary's Wharf and the other branching at Oviedo.

With surveyors out, a deal with a competing steamboat, rail delivered and some land bought, the Plant Railroad began to see that the pertinacious growers of Oviedo hadn't made idle threats, so they came down to seven cents per box, and this satisfied the majority of growers. Although the rails were sold for old iron, the cost reduction for orange shipping more than paid for the investment the growers put into the enterprise.

In the winter of 1889, Foster had an offer of $50,000 for his Gee Hammock Grove, which he refused. As the cash returns for his two groves were $20,000 in the following year, it seemed he'd made the right choice, but the freezes of 1894–95 killed his groves, making them near worthless. Asked if he regretted his refusal to sell out before the freeze, Foster replied, "Selling would only have shifted the loss upon another. In declining several tempting offers for both groves, I tried to use my best judgment, and I certainly sought God's direction. I must still feel I acted as God would have me."

While many of his northern friends abandoned the land, Foster continued to tend his groves and was still a part of the Oviedo community, coming back each winter until he was too ill to do so, dying in 1901.

PRINCE BUTLER BOSTON, AFTER THE BIG FREEZE

While most folks were scared off by the Big Freeze of 1894–95, one man got an opportunity to grow oranges near Oviedo because of it. His name was Prince Butler Boston, the son of Dr. Alexander Atkinson. Boston was one of three children the Dr. Alexander Atkinson fathered with two freed woman off of his family's plantation in Camden County, Georgia.

For the time, Oviedo was a fairly welcoming city for African Americans, so it makes sense that Dr. Atkinson would chose it as the place to bring his black twelve-year-old son in 1885. Atkinson came to the area to hang out a shingle as a doctor and druggist, as well as to buy three hundred acres of orange groves.

Some sources say that Dr. Atkinson was a black man, one of the first African American doctors to serve the area, but there's evidence that he might have been white—or, at the very least, attempted to be part of white society. In the census rolls of 1880, Dr. Atkinson is listed as white in his home county of Camden, Georgia.

Atkinson also attended First Baptist Church in Oviedo, a predominantly white church in the area, and he took his son with him when he was younger. Boston would later chose to go to Antioch Missionary Baptist Church as an adult, which was an African American church. On census rolls in 1920, Boston was listed as "mulatto," or mixed race. We do know, for certain, that Dr. Atkinson was the son of a slave owner. Boston's last name was one he chose, perhaps because he refused to continue carrying a family name with such a legacy.

After the Big Freeze, Dr. Atkinson decided to move, and he gave his son the gift of the ruined groves. Boston was in his twenties when his father gave him the acreage, and Boston had been five years married to Julia Johnson, with whom he would have ten children. Prince Butler Boston worked all sorts of jobs: bricklayer, carpenter, citrus grower and, most importantly, nursery man.

One story told of him was of the time that T.W. Lawton hired him to bud trees, directing Boston to bud half the trees. When Lawton came to inspect them, he found that all the trees had been budded, but only on one side— literally half of every tree in the grove. It's tough to say if this incident was just a simple misunderstanding or malicious compliance on Boston's part. From all accounts, though, Boston knew the citrus business well.

Lawton was a member of one of the leading white families in Oviedo (his family owned the general store, and he would later go on to become the superintendent of schools), and Boston eventually became a respected leader in the black community. Boston was registered to vote in a time when few African Americans were, became a deacon of his church for forty-five years and a local school trustee and would go on to encourage young black men in the community.

One of the young men he mentored described Boston as "the best conditioned man I ever knew," perhaps because he didn't tend to get angry about things he didn't approve of, responding with humor instead—as in the often-repeated story of the mule and the Ford truck. One day, his sons fell to cursing at a stubborn mule that just wouldn't plow a furrow, but Boston didn't chide them; he simply walked away. The next day, watching the same group of boys try in vain to start up the Ford truck, he turned to his wife and said, "Tell them to try the words they used on the mule."

Boston's family claim that his contributions to oranges were that he was the first to bud the Jamaica Temple Orange Trees and created the Boston Banana Orange. The Jamaica Temple Orange he introduced and budded for J.H. King and for J.H. Lee in Oviedo, but he didn't patent it, so he never got the credit, according to family history.

Although he died in 1947, Boston's legacy carries on today, some in the form of descendants, many of whom have gone on to work in education and community activism, as he did, but also in local place names in Oviedo: Boston Street, Boston Alley, Boston Cemetery and Boston Hill.

WHEELER'S FERTILIZER AND ORANGE INNOVATIONS

Another man who took the Big Freeze as an opportunity rather than a blow was Benjamin Franklin Wheeler. Florida-born, he came to his mother's hometown of Oviedo in 1889, working as a telegraph operator for the Atlantic Coast Line at the age of sixteen.

After the freezes left groves abandoned and the packinghouses empty, Wheeler bought a seedling grove and packinghouse in 1898, working the land when he wasn't at Atlantic Coast, budding some of the trees with Dancy tangerines. He was said to be the first to bud Navel and Valencia onto Cleo rootstock (short for Cleopatra Mandarin). He also planted celery, after the 1917 freeze schooled him in the ways of diversification beyond citrus.

He partnered up with Nelson Brothers Packinghouse in 1908, buying out one partner in 1913, and by 1923, he'd bought out the rest, giving him sole ownership of the business. The packinghouse was one of the first to use water-based wax and fungicides.

Almost by accident, he founded the Wheeler Fertilizer Company in 1932. Farmers in the 1930s began to use fertilizer at a much higher rate, seeing that it benefited their yields and quality greatly, as they followed seasonal guides from the Lake Alfred Citrus Experiment Station. As Wheeler had plenty of land to work, he bought his in bulk through a wholesaler, keeping a supply on hand in a warehouse. Other farmers in the area knew of this stockpile, so when they ran low, they bought small amounts from Wheeler, and they soon realized that it was a good way to get fertilizer when they needed it, instead of waiting on orders by train. Wheeler began buying more to keep up with demand and eventually just turned it into a business. Harry Hasson, one of his employees, then suggested that instead of ordering wholesale, they should mix their own, so Wheeler took his suggestion, opening a plant and experimenting with different mixes for different types of crops, establishing the use of dolomite as the most cost-effective way to get magnesium into a grove. When he was woken with the news of his fertilizer plant having burned to the ground in 1947, his first reaction was that of concern for the farmers, saying, "What will happen to the growers?" He rebuilt the enterprise in six months.

Water conservation also interested Wheeler, and he discovered how best to use drainage wells to that end and drain tiles to hold the water at the correct level for the best production of citrus. His other innovations include being one of the first in Central Florida to use a hedging machine on his orange trees and, as of 1940, being the first in Seminole and East Orange Counties to bud Orlando Tangelos on Cleo and Sour Orange rootstock.

Wheeler married Georgia Lee near the start of his career in 1908. She, a staunch Methodist, did not join his Baptist church, but neither did he join hers. She continued to spend her Sundays on Methodist ground, taking their daughters with her, while he still went to the Oviedo First Baptist Church, taking their son with him. B.F. Wheeler acted as deacon and Sunday school superintendent for more than thirty years. After his death, his family found that he'd been supporting a missionary in Africa for more than a decade.

Politically active, Wheeler served as Seminole County commissioner and on Oviedo City Council and helped found the Seminole County Chamber of Commerce. He also served as a member of the Advisory Council of Stetson University, as well as a trustee of Bob Jones University.

His storied citrus résumé contains lots of involvement with various organizations. As one of the original organizers of Florida Citrus Mutual, besides the packinghouse and the fertilizer business, he also partially owned a citrus concentrate plant, was director of a canning operation, held a pivotal role in developing the Citrus Inspection Service and helped organize the Ocklawaha Citrus Processing Co-op. He saw the need for the co-op because after World War II, when the government dropped its citrus contracts, growers had been planting to supply them, and the market was glutted. By organizing the co-op, he helped seventeen fresh fruit shippers to sign contracts with several concentrate plants. He also started the Citizen's Bank of Oviedo for the farmers of Seminole County, serving as bank's president until his death in 1954.

His son, B.F. Wheeler Jr., carried on the family tradition of citrus. Jr. continued to innovate in citrus, fertilizers and other enterprises until his death in 2006.

The Florida State Commerce Building dedicated a chair to Wheeler Sr. in recognition for his leadership in the citrus industry, and the Florida Citrus Hall of Fame inducted him in 1997.

SEMINOLE COUNTY IN THE LAST CENTURY THROUGH TODAY

The freezes of the 1910s were still fresh in the minds of growers when disaster struck in the late 1920s with the discovery of the Mediterranean fruit fly near Orlando. The Department of Agriculture imposed a quarantine from April 1929 to the fall of 1929, which didn't hit in the thickest part of production (November–February) but probably did make the growers here even more cautious about counting on citrus or any fruit.

Celery, first planted in Sanford, spread all over the county, especially in the Oviedo area. Between Lake Jesup and Oviedo lay Black Hammock lands, drained by 1915 for muck farming. Oranges and citrus could make you a profit, but growers in Seminole were learning not to count on it as their sole source of income through the century of 1900.

Around World War II, grower Frank Wheeler (aka B.F. Wheeler Jr.) remembered the Seaboard Train being loaded up for Winter Park and then on to Orlando "40 or 50 cars of celery on the train every night," and the Coastline Train, he said, would have fifteen to twenty cars of citrus or celery on it five nights a week.

By the 1950s, strain on the water table, with the demand of so many residents, began the problem of saltwater intrusion, an issue for residents and farms, especially those who counted on wells for their water supply. There's been further study and stopgap solutions since the 1980s, but it is still a difficulty for some parts of the county. Water conservation here and in other parts of the state has led to many papers and studies from Lake Alfred researchers. The CREC launched a water reclamation program in 1986—the Water Conserv II project, the largest citrus water reclamation program in the world.

The 1970s saw the county shipping more than two thousand freight car loads of celery and citrus, probably more celery than citrus by that time.

Today, past disasters such as Hurricane Donna in 1960, the Med-fly in the '30s, outbreaks of canker and all the freezes from 1900 to the 1980s and beyond have dwindled the number of oranges grown in county, as growers move on to other parts of the state or give up altogether.

As of the 2015–16 Florida Department of Agriculture report, Seminole County ships only forty-three thousand citrus boxes, thirty-seven thousand of which are oranges, placing them in the lowest tier of orange growing for the state. For the year, this accounts for under 0.05 percent of orange production in the state. Of the citrus producing counties in the state, only Citrus and Putnam Counties were lower than Seminole. Still, citrus can be found in the form of Red Hill Groves in Sanford at its farm store, where it sells orange juice, ice cream, onions and grove fresh oranges when they're in season.

THE RIDGE

The Ridge is a geographical feature of Florida on which many oranges have been grown. When growers speak of growing areas, it's Indian River, the 'Glades—which are really South Florida groves, whether they touch the Everglades or not—and the Ridge. Outside the world of citrus, this geographical feature is known as the Mid-Florida Ridge or the Lake Wales Ridge.

The Ridge stretches a long 115 miles in Central Florida, although some estimates have it at an even more impressive 150 miles. For a native of the state, used to flat lands at or below sea level, the Ridge might as well be a mountain, but for those from mountainous areas it probably qualifies as a hill, although it varies in height from place to place. But it is a very long hill, a sort of spine across miles of Central Florida. Beginning at Leesburg in Lake County just south of Lake Harris, it runs south to Sebring in Highlands County, running through Polk County. No bigger than twenty-five miles across, at times it narrows to just a mile. Most of the Ridge's land can be found in Lake, Polk and Highlands Counties, with smaller sections in Orange and Osceola Counties to the east and patch in the far northwest corner of Hardee County. At its tallest point, it's about three hundred feet.

In its early history, the Ridge was just a chain of islands, sand dunes formed by the currents of the Gulf of Mexico and the Atlantic Ocean. The Ridge has its origins in the Pleistocene, a geological epoch from about 2,588,000 to 11,700 years ago. Had you stood on the center of the Ridge then, you would have been surrounded on two sides by seawater, as most of the rest of

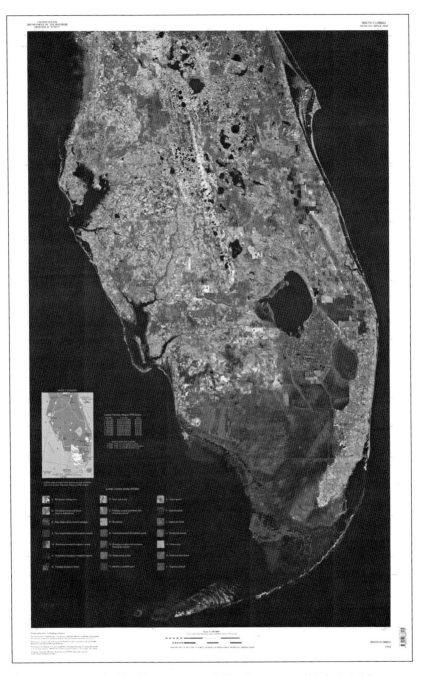

Satellite image of Florida. You can see the Ridge from space! *U.S. Geological Survey, Department of the Interior/USGS.*

Florida was covered in water. After the Pleistocene, it was further heightened by geologic movement.

In more modern times, the height and good drainage of the Ridge makes for excellent orange land, although the sands need added fertilizer and the sometimes desert-like conditions mean that irrigation is a must. The heat reflects off the sands, but the limestone underneath means sinkholes, some of which have formed into the many Ridge-top lakes, oases of coolness.

Author John McPhee noted the instability of the Ridge in the 1960s when he wrote of the conditions he saw in the groves, describing one of the sinkholes as one hundred feet across and forty feet deep, where "Valencia trees around the rim tilted crazily over the edge, part of their roots protruding into the air, bleached white by the sun." The limestone bed that the sand lies on can give way, sometimes because a fissure forms and sand pours through it, making a hole, because the drained limestone caverns can no longer support the sandy roof.

In the more natural and preserved parts of the Ridge, you'll find a unique scrub habitat, supporting rarities such as the Florida scrub-jay, gopher tortoises, the only sand swimming skink in North America and other species that are rare or endangered. In many areas, the sands are a pristine white, and walking across them feels a lot like a trek through dunes at the beach. That's really what the Ridge is—an ancient sand dune, marooned smack dab in the middle of the state. Even with all the rain Florida gets, the Ridge

Bluetail mole skink in Highlands County. *Glenn Bartolotti, 2015.*

can get dry enough to tax plants, especially since water drains quickly from the sands—unlike more organic soil, it doesn't retain moisture well. You'll find plants such as the prickly pear cactus and the sand live oak, its thick and leathery leaves rolled up at the edges to retain moisture.

As of 2007, Lake and Orange Counties had greater proportions of residential zones on the Ridge than Polk County, with development and other uses overtaking citrus in Lake and Orange. With its unique ecological value, in places where it hasn't been converted to pine growing, oranges or residential, we've sought to preserve it as a natural habitat. While you won't find any oranges in the scrublands, you might find plants and animals unique to the scrub's desert-like conditions. There are a number of places in Highlands and Polk Counties where you can hike the Ridge, and you can learn more about the plant life at Bok Tower Gardens. Managed natural areas include Lake Kissimmee State Park, Crooked Lake Prairie, the Lake Wales Ridge State Forest/Walk-in-Water Tract, Archbold Biological Station, Lake June-in-Winter Scrub State Park, Tiger Creek Preserve and Pine Ridge Nature Preserve. If you want to visit a Ridge grove, try Ridge Island Groves in Haines City—during the season it gives tours.

EARLY GROWTH OF POLK COUNTY

The history of oranges in Polk County could fill a book of its own, as there are many luminaries of the groves who came out of Polk and many important discoveries made there, especially at the Lake Alfred Citrus Experimental Station, which just celebrated its one-hundred-year anniversary. The orange history in Polk County reflected much of what was happening overall in the state, most definitely in Central Florida.

Polk has long been a major producer of citrus in Florida, and it still is today. It's the leader in orange production for Central Florida.

During the 1880s, the state contracted with the industrialist Hamilton Disston to drain the swamplands in neighboring counties, east of Peace River and just north of Kissimmee, but Disston showed interest in Polk County, eventually buying up 102,000 acres of land through his Florida Land and Improvement Company. Disston was from Philadelphia, but his connections with English investors, along with those of Sir Edward Reed's, helped to sell land in Polk and Osceola Counties to Englishmen. They also advertised in papers across the nation, their efforts more than doubling the population in Polk between 1880 and 1885, up to 6,623 people.

There was one area of Central Florida groves during the little freezes of the late 1880s that by some quirk survived the cold with no damage in Polk County. On the higher sandhills of Keystone City, Joe Carson, from one of the founding families of the city, noticed that those orange trees were more resistant to the frosts than low-lying trees. Keystone was a young city, and the postal service rejected the name because there was already Keystone Heights registered. The postmaster, W.H. Overocker, asked the citizens to submit a new name so they could open a post office. They settled on Lakemont, but Carson, who had just gotten his real estate license, thought to name it Frostproof, to better market the area to orange growers. Overruled on the choice of name, Carson then very nicely volunteered to hand deliver the application. Unbeknownst to Overocker, Carson took the opportunity to change the name on the application, so the city became Frostproof, and as residents wanted the post office open as soon as possible, Overocker decided it would be too much trouble to apply to change the name to Lakemont.

Once the freezes of the late 1890s hit, the lie of the city's name embarrassed residents since the frosts had hit the groves there just as hard as they had elsewhere. They had the name changed to Lakemont in 1897, only to have Carson successfully campaign to change it back again in 1906. As the determined Carson was quoted as saying, "A thousand other places have names beginning with 'Lake.' There is but one Frostproof in the known world."

Before the Big Freezes of 1894–95, although Polk's fortunes were already starting to wane due to the Panic of 1893, they did better than most orange areas when the freeze hit because they had other major businesses to fall back on: phosphates and lumber. In any case, they were probably the first county to rebound in the citrus industry itself, for by 1913 Polk was leading the state in citrus production.

POLK COUNTY AND THE LAND BOOM YEARS, 1910–26

South Florida saw the most action in real estate during the Florida Land Boom, but Central Florida had its fair share, bringing in buyers by the trainload as the binder boys laid in wait. Binder boys (of which a scattered few were women) would sell the right to buy a piece of land to prospective buyers, asking for a binder fee paid only to hold the land, with the actual land price due within thirty days. At the height of the craze in Florida, they would often sell the binder on the spot, without the client even having seen the land, because the demand was so strong that buyers thought it more prudent to secure the right to buy than wait to see it. A picture of Polk County's Haven Villa Corporation salesforce showed more than one hundred people crowded into the wide shot in 1925.

In the 1910s and 1920s, during the thick of the Florida Land Boom, W.J. Howey (later to be the founder of Howey-in-the-Hills) ran a "Land Seekers Special" via the railroad to Dundee. Howey would sometimes hire an entire train to get his prospective buyers in, refunding their fare from the north if they bought property with him.

The orange business at the time wasn't just limited to the fruit. In Polk, nurseries were also big business. No matter where you were growing in the state from 1910 to 1920, chances were you got your tree or buds from one of the many nurseries in the county. The most well-known was Glen St. Mary Nursery Company, established in 1882. It was the new land they bought in 1912 near Dundee, where they would go on to sell some of the more well-known varieties of oranges and citrus of the time (such as the Lue Gim Gong). Throughout the twentieth century on through to today, they've supplied everyone from wholesalers and commercial growers to home gardeners and enthusiasts with stock, citrus and otherwise.

Citrus concerns large and small brought money to the county, but the most successful were careful to have their fortunes tied up in more than one enterprise. Latimer "Latt" Maxcy of Frostproof, for instance, had his hand in cattle, fruit, fertilizer and vegetable farming.

While there were orange cultivators before Maxcy, his legend was such that he was known as the first orange grower in Frostproof, a complete fiction, as he got his start convincing his father to buy land in the early 1900s and he only bought land starting in 1914, long after the city got its name in the late 1800s. But he had a significant impact on Florida oranges of the twentieth century, both in Polk and Osceola Counties.

Maxcy opened Lake Reedy Packing Company near Frostproof in 1917, later closing that and opening the more impactful Latt Maxcy Inc. in 1925. By 1931, it had become the largest packing concern in the area. He also owned canning facilities. While he made his mark in citrus, Maxcy diversified as a major cattle farmer and fertilizer producer.

Besides innovations in canning and other areas of citrus, he is also credited with forming the cooperative Florida Citrus Mutual in 1948, along with James C. Morton and A.B. Michael, where he served as the organization's first president. The co-op membership of Florida Citrus Mutual would later boast more than twelve thousand growers.

POLK COUNTY LAND BUST AND THE GREAT DEPRESSION, 1926–40

When the Florida Land Boom went bust in 1926, Polk continued to prosper—or at least hold steady in a slow decline. South Florida, which didn't have much else going on, suffered a total collapse, but most (though not all) of the promised building projects in Polk carried on. This was true of other Central Florida counties—Lake County, where Howey founded Howey-in-the-Hills, continued to sell land, albeit at a less frenetic rate, until the Great Depression pushed it further into the doldrums. Evidence of the unfulfilled grandiose promises of the Florida Land Boom, such as the uncompleted "Skeleton Hotel" in Fort Meade, could be found among the hard-won successes, but compared to the rest of the country, most of Polk County was better off during the height of the Great Depression.

After Florida Land Boom, when the Great Depression hit other counties hard, the many industries in Polk significantly softened the blow. According to the *Florida Municipal Record* at the time, Polk was the "richest per-capita county in the U.S." That's not to say there weren't poor folks in Polk at the time, but there were certainly far fewer of them than there were in other parts of the country.

Besides citrus, lumber mills, turpentine, phosphates, cattle and farming, the newest saving grace for the county was tourism. The railway in the area had become firmly established by the 1920s, but it was the "Good Roads" movement that literally paved the way for the "tin-can tourists" who motored their way into the county for decades after. These tourists didn't have the deepest pockets, staying in tents and trailers rather than hotels, but their sheer numbers helped buoy the county further. By 1920, Polk had probably the best road system in the state and, as the slogan for the Good Roads project noted, "a road from every town in Polk County to every other town!"

Groves and orange culture were a big part of what tourists came to see in Polk, and the cities there were happy to oblige. In 1924, Winter Haven held the first Orange Festival. By late 1937, the city was rushing to finish permanent buildings constructed especially for the 1938 festival. It had even hired a muralist from Tampa to illustrate the walls. According to contemporaneous accounts, the Queen of the Orange Festival had no fewer than six ladies as her "court of honor."

Times in Polk were less difficult than elsewhere during the Depression, but it wasn't untouched. Labor workers on the lower scale of things could find jobs, but since workers were going where the work was (and Polk had more work than most) local workers, including those of the orange groves, found themselves competing with the desperate from other places. That, coupled with the falling prices of oranges, made the rate paid to the workers low, even comparable to other jobs.

Citrus workers pushed for National Recovery Administration involvement, hoping that enrollment in the New Deal program would bring up wages and help conditions, but the growers refused. And so, a union, United Citrus Workers, formed in the early 1930s, but their power fizzled out due to threats from growers, and because conditions slightly improved by the mid-1930s.

FROM HARD TIMES TO THE BEST TIMES IN POLK, 1940–70

It might be better said that Polk didn't dodge the Great Depression—it just came later and slower for the county. While other places in the United States were on the upswing in the late 1930s and 1940s, the hard times had finally worn the county down. The start of the war in late 1941 didn't help either—businesses that had been keeping labor on during the hard times of the Depression found that war was another matter entirely, so a good many people were out of work.

Citrus growers hadn't been entirely savvy, and in the late 1930s, supply outstripped the demand. This led to the formation of co-ops as growers sought new markets, but the world war in Europe made that difficult.

Once the United States entered the war, everything changed again with the glut of fruit suddenly wanted by the U.S. government to provide vitamin C to the troops. And it wasn't just American needs being fulfilled. From 1942 to 1943, 1 million gallons of orange juice came out of the Lake Wales–based Florida Citrus Canners Cooperative for use in the United Kingdom under Roosevelt's lend-lease program.

World War II began orange juice concentrate development mainly because of government needs, but at the war's end, growers now had a product they wanted to promote to regular consumers, and in 1945 they began marketing and selling frozen concentrate in commercial markets.

The war's end wasn't the end of orange juice's relationship with the federal government, of course, and a 1946 school lunch program proved an ideal way for the growers of Polk to sell surplus juice.

If ever we could say there was a heyday for oranges in Florida, it would have to be from after World War II through the 1960s. By 1950, Polk County was growing more oranges than any other county in the United States except Orange County, California. There was money to be made, especially after a Texas drought lessened the supply, pushing the price of oranges up. The trouble was that people knew there was money to be made in Florida, so in 1954, the state found itself with the problem of oversupply once again.

But the concentrate market pushed a boom, as growers began improving the taste and marketing concentrate to home consumers, to excellent effect. Florida production of frozen concentrate jumped from 226,000 gallons in 1946 to a huge increase by 1962 with more than 116 million concentrate gallons.

Opportunities for the shrewd, especially those who had established themselves in the orange business, were ripe for the picking. Latt Maxcy, for instance, benefited from the boom in citrus of the 1920s, but he also weathered the Great Depression and the glut of citrus in the 1930s and early '40s before cashing in on the concentrate age in a big, big way. Maxcy merged his groves with Snow Crop, the frozen foods division of Clinton Foods, which handled orange concentrate. When Snow Crop sold to Minute Maid, Maxcy made a bundle, an estimated $5 million.

POLK'S DECLINE, BUT STILL STRONG, 1970s–PRESENT

Oranges have faced many crises throughout their cultivation in Florida—fruit flies, spreading decline, citrus canker, hurricanes, today's citrus greening and much more—but the constant worry for the Central Florida grove grower has been the freezes. And the freezes in the 1970s and early 1980s led to some growers shifting buying up property in counties more Southwest than Central in the state.

Anyone alive in Florida in the 1980s cannot help but recall the dire laments of the nightly news as the groves froze, plaguing growers various years throughout the decade, finally culminating in the most terrible freeze in a terrible decade of freezes: the 1989 freeze.

Frank Hunt III, a third-generation grower out of Lake Wales in Polk County, had this to say in a *Southeast Farm Press* article: "If we hadn't had that South Florida acreage after the '89 freeze, we'd probably have gone out of business. That saved Hunt Bros."

The Hunt Bros. wasn't the only citrus concern that shifted elsewhere. Paul Meador, himself a third-generation orange grower, moved down to LaBelle, Florida, in the 1970s. Ben Hill Griffin Jr. planted 1,450 acres in Charlotte County and 1,500 in Hendry County in the late '80s.

So the crown Polk wore so well for so many years as Citrus Queen of Florida toppled off, as Southwest counties came for it. The year 1992 saw St. Lucie County take the crown, and then, in 1995, Polk slipped to the number three spot, with Lucie first and Hendry second in citrus production. Although Hendry was second, it was first as far as orange production specifically was concerned.

Despite the slips of the crown, Polk's orange industry has stayed strong relative to the rest of the state, a bastion of Central Florida orange growing. In the 2015–16 season, the county was the third-largest producer of citrus with 12,539,000 boxes, behind DeSoto County (12,773,000 boxes) and the leader of Hendry with 14,282,000 boxes. For the 2016–17 season, Polk inched up in production by comparison, back up to the number two spot for both overall citrus and in oranges. Some seasons, like 2014–15, it's back up to its supreme slot, as the top producer of oranges and citrus.

THE GRIFFIN ORANGE DYNASTY IN FROSTPROOF AND BEYOND

Talking to the larger growers, it's not uncommon to find folks who have citrus in their family several generations back. One such family is the Griffins.

Ben Hill Griffin Jr., born in the midst of a hurricane in 1910, began the family legacy in earnest, although his father had also been a keeper of groves and gifted to his son ten acres of oranges near Frostproof as a wedding present. Griffin Jr. had grown up tending his father's groves, doing everything from spraying the groves in a mule cart to spreading fertilizer, pruning, hoeing and shimmying up trees to get oranges pickers had missed (known in the grove business as shiners for their tendency to shine brightly orange and catch attention). His first wage-paying job was at the L. Maxcy Company's fresh-fruit packinghouse.

Griffin tended his own acreage, but he also picked up jobs managing other groves, putting the money earned into buying more land and planting more citrus. By the early 1940s, he'd acquired thousands of acres—the sixteen-thousand-acre Peace River Ranch and a fifty-five-thousand-acre ranch in Highlands County, Florida. Smart enough to diversify, he also used his land for other enterprises—cattle and timber.

Seizing opportunity when he saw it, he snatched up a concentrate plant and even more land in the late 1950s, when Minute Maid sold off property as a result of an antitrust case.

In John McPhee's *Oranges*, which covers the author's travels through Florida orange lands in 1965, many of the orange growers and pomologists continually recommended he speak with Griffin Jr., as they felt he was the last of the true "orange barons" in the state, and Griffin even owned his own juice processing plant and company, later acquired by P&G, which became Citrus Hill in 1982.

Where Griffin Jr.'s father had given ten acres of citrus, Griffin III got a different kind of gift from his father, not as a wedding gift but upon graduation from high school: one hundred shares of his father's company, Alico. Like his father, Griffin III was a leader in the citrus industry, serving on many boards with distinction. From 1990 to 2004, Griffin III presided as president and chairman of the Alico Inc. board, and the company's assets reached a record $176.9 million.

Griffin III also worked to promote Florida oranges outside of Florida and supported the University of Florida's Institute of Food and Agricultural Sciences' efforts to solve citrus industry challenges.

Today, Griffin III's son, Ben Hill Griffin IV, has carried on in the family tradition of orange growing. In an interview with Florida's Natural (an all-Florida orange juice co-op that Griffin IV is part of), when asked what the family secret was to success in the citrus business, he answered, "My grandfather and father taught me early on that as a citrus grower, there will be good years and not-so-good years. High fruit prices followed by low prices. Pest and disease challenges, etc. Every year will be different. Perseverance is part of the job description."

ORANGE COUNTY IN BRIEF

Orange County's history of oranges and other citrus parallels a lot of Central Florida, but Orange County stands out from other Central Florida counties for a few reasons: more development and higher real estate prices at crucial points, mainly because of Disney World. The development makes it much more like Southeast Florida than Central Florida in respect to citrus today.

Citrus growing doesn't happen in a vacuum. Groves compete for land with other enterprises, be they cattle in counties such as Osceola and Polk, celery in Seminole or, in the case of Orange County, high real estate demand driven by tourism. The moment it became known that Disney was behind the mysterious buy-ups of land, real estate prices skyrocketed, so many orange growers cashed out even as early as 1965, before the park was even completed in 1971.

In the 2016–17 season, just 149,000 boxes of oranges were produced in the county that was named for them. To put that in perspective, 68,750,000 boxes of oranges were produced for the State of Florida, meaning that roughly .002 percent of oranges in Florida come from Orange County.

Just .002 percent of the state's orange crop is quite a drop from what it used to be. Through to the 1950s, Orange County lived up to its name. True, it trailed Polk County by quite a lot, but it was the second-highest producer of oranges in the state for decades.

There are many place names within the county reflective of its citrus heritage—not the least of which was the Citrus Bowl, changed to Camping World Stadium in 2017. Considering how little citrus comes out of Orange County these days, it's perhaps apt, but as one *Orlando Sentinel* reporter put it, "Now that the Citrus Bowl will be erased from maps, the last big landmark and homage to the industry that gave the county its name is gone. The passing wasn't a sudden one. Citrus has been on its way out for decades. But watching the Citrus Bowl name get the boot is kind of like seeing the name of someone you know in the obituaries. It makes it real."

DR. PHILIP PHILLIPS

It's a name you remember once you've heard it. Dr. Philip Phillips became an orange baron in Central Florida from the 1920s to the 1950s, most specifically in Orange County, Florida. He grew up in Tennessee, born to French parents, and got his doctoral degree in New York City. But he decided not to make his fortune as a doctor. He began in Putnam County, growing citrus near the city of Satsuma, finding bitter disappointment once the Big Freezes of 1894–95 killed his groves. Seemingly defeated, he went back to Tennessee. But he wasn't done with Florida and kept coming back for visits in the post-freeze 1890s, buying up land.

Cuba in 1902 was his next stop, but the political instability there gave him pause, so he came back to Florida. He'd had a short stint caring for groves in the early 1900s near Kissimmee, but he settled in Orlando and Orange County about 1905 near Sand Lake, establishing trees that stood until the early 1960s, when a hospital was built on the land.

Phillips's impact will largely be remembered in Orange County, but he acquired land all around Central Florida, becoming a bonafide orange

A fruit delivery truck dated from Dr. Phillips's golden age, between 1920 and 1950. *Dr. Phillips Charities Collection.*

baron before the advent of World War II. He'd bought up enough land that even before the 1910s, he'd become an important figure in the citrus industry.

Phillips liked data, so heading up the statistics committee of the Florida Horticultural Society was a good fit for him, and in 1907, after roving over the entire state talking to farmers, he gave reports as to the condition of citrus in each county and estimates of percentage of the various kinds grown—what percentage grapefruit or oranges, as well as the total boxes harvested. The work took him all over the state, probably presenting him with even more opportunities, not just to learn what grew best where but also what land he might buy. At its height in the 1920s and '30s, his agricultural business sold 100 million oranges per year, more than any other citrus business in the world at the time.

Immediately around the grove near Sand Lake, he bought huge tracts, his groves stretching vast over eighteen square miles in Orange County. All the people needed for the working of it eventually formed a little village of sorts, called Dr. Phillips after the grove magnate. Today, it's a suburb of Orlando.

Originally Orlando Regional Sand Lake Hospital, where his first groves were planted in 1907, renamed Dr. P. Phillips Hospital in his honor (2007), in the Dr. Phillips suburb of Orlando. *By Visitor7, Wikimedia Commons.*

His thirst for data and a scientific mind likely contributed to his innovations in the orange business, which ranged from selling citrus by the pound to using airplanes to spray pesticides on his groves. His largest contribution was researching and marketing a palatable orange juice in the early days of the business.

In about 1929, Phillips brought a team together to build a market for, and experiment with, canned juice. Discovering a "flash" pasteurization process that improved on the taste of former versions, the doctor began a marketing blitz across five states. The slogan "Drink Dr. Phillips' orange juice because the Doc says it's good for you!" appeared on his juice products.

Like Latt Maxcy, Phillips cashed in at the right time, selling the majority of his holdings to Granada Groves and Minute Maid for a massive profit in 1953, widely believed to be the largest deal in the history of citrus during that time. Dr. Phillips passed away just six years later at eighty-five years old. His son Howard got the business, but his other son, Walter, also worked in citrus as a consultant. When Howard died, much of his fortune largely went to charity, something Dr. Phillips would have wanted as he supported charity and the arts all of his life. His legacy lives on through his charitable foundations.

SOUTHERNMOST CENTRAL FLORIDA

Highlands and Hardee Counties, nestled just underneath Polk County, are the two most southerly counties of what's considered Central Florida. In the 2016–17 season, both Hardee and Highlands Counties were in the top five citrus producing counties in Florida. Their current ranking reflects a more southern shift in orange-growing, although historically in the twentieth century, both counties were high to mid-range in overall ranking for orange growing.

Valencia oranges for juicing are mainly grown in Highlands and Hardee today, as is true for the rest of the state. In the past, there were many more varieties grown—and in 1908, one such was developed west of Waluscha in Hardee County. Albert Carlton's tree bore fruit nearly without seeds, described thusly by an historian: "The fruit was of medium size, almost perfectly round, with a thin velvety skin. The pulp was of a deep yellow color and the fruit was sweet and of exquisite flavor." The fruit was known by two different names: "Fancy Golden Bright" and the "Carlton Seedless." Though distributed far and wide via nurseries, it's not prevalent today. What can be found today are the Carltons themselves, an old Florida family who have been farming and ranching throughout Florida since the late 1800s. Dennis Carlton is mostly out of Hillsborough County, ranches cattle, and has been replacing some of his citrus with strawberries because of citrus greening. The Doyle Carlton branch of the family has been ranching cattle for several generations and still sells beef today.

The southern end of the Ridge comes across Highlands, ending in Sebring, Florida. Because the Ridge in this area hasn't been as developed agriculturally or residentially as Polk, much of it has been devoted to conservation efforts.

The general orange shift to the Highlands and Hardee happened in the late 1950s. The more northern parts of the Ridge had suffered from outbreaks of nematodes, and the more northern counties had also had freezes to contend with, as well as land shortages. A bitter freeze in the 1957–58 season continued the move south; although Hardee and Highlands had both been consistent producers of citrus before that, after that point they became even more prevalent as more and more orange growers bought up land.

CENTRAL FLORIDA, PAST AND PRESENT

Central Florida is one of two areas with the richest history of orange cultivation in the state, along with the Indian River or Central East Coast area. While Central Florida squeezes a large percentage of Valencias for juice, it also carries on the tradition of selling whole oranges to the public. There are more places for the culinary tourist to connect with orange culture here, as opposed to the newer and more industrially commercial orange operations of Florida's Southwest region.

SUNSHINE IN A GLASS

I n the iconography of Florida oranges in the last century, there's nothing more central than a glass of Florida orange juice. To picture the first citrus juice processing plant in Florida, you'd have to go back to Haines City in 1915, when cars were an eccentricity and roads were more often dust than pavement. On the topmost floor, workers halved grapefruit, placing the halves fruit side down on an extractor. The juice collection methods used gravity, the juice running down to the lowest floor, into their bottles, and labeled Street's Pure Grapefruit Juice. The quart glass bottles left the plant in horse-drawn carts, clinking in their wooden cases to be delivered to the railway station.

High freight costs, poor shelf life and the First World War ended the venture, but the logistical citrus juicing knowledge won at the plant during the tenure of Street and others at the building would serve the orange industry well in later years. Street's son, C.C. Street, said that "the most basic knowledge of citrus processing and later canning was developed" at the facility.

The Polk Canning Company took over the building in 1916, with all of its equipment powered entirely by steam, save for the electric lights. Its business centered more on canning and less on juice, but it took a few years for it to get the tin cans formulated for citrus. The acidity of citrus tends to quickly rust most metal, so this was invaluable when the industry began canning concentrate. R.L. Polk Sr. said they shipped the first carload of tinned citrus by train in the fall of 1921.

At the peak of its operations in the 1930s, the Polk Canning Company employed eight hundred people. The building would stand until the late twentieth century, and before that, Suni Citrus used it as a lab, storage facility and offices, starting in the 1950s.

If you've a tendency to think of bygone days as better than modern times in every aspect, a sip of commercial orange juice in the 1930s might dispel that notion. Basically, it was boiled orange juice, which was then canned. As oranges have a complex, volatile flavor profile, the concoction was nothing like a fresh-squeezed orange. Depending on the process used, it might have tasted like vaguely flavored sugar water with just a touch of turpentine.

But there were important advancements made in the 1920s and '30s. William John Howey, founder of Howey-in-the-Hills, sold juice at his many land-sales office locations across the country and in Florida as a way to buoy sagging profits because of the Florida Land Boom Bust and the Great Depression. For maximum profit, he opened his own juice processing plant and developed a quick electric pasteurization technique, one of the first in the state to do so.

Orange juice, even as far back as the early 1900s, benefited from an image as a healthful beverage, with some researchers claiming that orange juice could help combat "Acidosis," a condition discredited as highly uncommon by the 1930s. Next, juice promoters touted vitamin C as the new panacea, a tactic that's alive and well today.

In the '30s and '40s, one of the pioneers of this healthful image was Dr. Philip Phillips. He used his position as a doctor to endorse his own product,

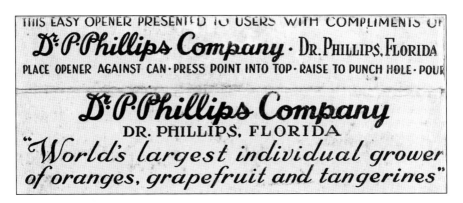

A box that originally held a can opener marketed along with Dr. Phillips's Canned Juices. *Dr. Phillips Charities Collection.*

emblazoning his juice products with the slogan "Drink Dr. Phillips' orange juice because the Doc says it's good for you." Phillips's claims spurred the American Medical Association to conduct a study on the healthfulness of oranges. Once the AMA released its positive report on orange juice, the boost in sales caused growers to pay attention. Phillips also won out by getting an AMA endorsement on every label.

Growers began to convert the juice into concentrated form in the 1930s, shipping out concentrate from California and Florida to the Midwest, but there was still a problem of palatability. The technique used to create concentrate was evaporation and lost much of the flavor. It came in mainly shelf-stable form.

FROM WORLD WAR II TO 1959

World War II spurred researchers into the next developments in orange juice. Vitamin C could ward off scurvy and other health issues, so rations for American soldiers included lemon crystals. Unfortunately, the crystals shared the problem of the juice and concentrate of the time: terrible taste. It did the troops no good if they refused to imbibe the source of the vitamin, so the Florida Department of Citrus began to develop something more delicious.

Just prior to the war, growers had been getting more and more efficient when it came to yields, as the science of fertilizer was more understood. The very thing that the promotional pamphlets of the 1800s had claimed would never happen had come to pass: an oversupply of oranges.

The war brought them government contracts, and these large deals saved the industry. But by the war's end, orange growers were again facing the problem of oversupply. Worse still, too many groves had been set out to fulfill contracts that expired once the war was over.

It wasn't until toward the end of the war, in 1945, that Louis G. Macdowell, Edwin L. Moore and Cedric D. Atkins, working for the Citrus Experiment Station at Lake Alfred, filed their patent, fulfilling the government's request for a more delicious concentrate.

Since converting juice into concentrate stripped it of essential flavors, the solution was a simple one: adding fresh, regular-strength orange juice back into concentrate, in a percentage of no more than 25 percent or less than 6 percent of the juice.

By 1948, manufacturers were adding the element of freezing concentrate, and Florida citrus growers finally had a marketable product.

Bing Crosby at a rubber scrap drive during World War II. *Franklin D. Roosevelt Library, Public Domain Photographs, U.S. National Archives and Records Administration.*

Unfortunately, those who'd served during World War II remembered the horrible stuff they'd tasted in the military. To convince the American public to drink orange juice, specifically concentrate, the industry needed a bold PR move, and in 1948, Minute Maid found the answer in the dulcet tones of Bing Crosby.

Minute Maid got into the frozen concentrate game in 1945, opening Florida's first frozen concentrate plant for $2.3 million in Plymouth, Florida. Without a large advertising budget, it lost $450,262 the first two years. In the spring of 1948, over a round of golf, John Hay Whitney, who had invested in Minute Maid (which then worked under the name Vacuum Foods Corp), talked Bing Crosby into representing the company and Crosby agreed to plug the product on his radio show. He would appear in orange juice ads for more than three decades.

Birds Eye, Snow Crop and others began to put out their own frozen concentrate. Minute Maid's sales increased so much that it earned $179,865 in the fiscal year of 1947–48, turning a profit for the first time. Demand was so high that Florida couldn't quite fill its needs, and it began looking into setting up plants in California.

In 1949, Florida's orange processing plants produced about 10 million gallons of concentrated orange juice, and American consumers enthusiastically bought the product. Citrus growers in Florida, such as Latimer "Latt" Maxcy in Polk County and Dr. Philip Phillips in Orange County, cashed in big time, selling their acreage to frozen concentrate corporations for millions in the 1950s.

Having experienced what bad buzz did to the industry before the late '40s ad blitz, industry grading of citrus juice was crucial to the reputation of American, in particular Florida juice. So the Florida Citrus Commission set standards to earn its seal of approval. In a 1959 court case, *Osceola Fruit Distributors v. Mayo*, we can see the lengths the state went to ensure standards and what a juice factory might do to cheat the system. Inspectors measured for sugar content, looked for additives, determined the orange oil percentage and amount of citric acid. On the basis of one hundred points, said one inspector called to testify, "you have a set number of points that you score juices for flavor; a set number for color, and whether or not there are defects present." The last grading criteria, color, was the one that Osceola Fruit Distributors tried to get around by adding dye to its blended orange and grapefruit drink. This earned Distributors a suspension of its certificate of registration and the citrus fruit dealer's license for fourteen days. The Florida Citrus Commission still sets standards today for any citrus product processed in the state containing more than 20 percent citrus.

THE HEIGHT OF THE FROZEN CONCENTRATE CRAZE

Finding fresh-squeezed Florida orange juice in the mid-1960s wasn't easy. In John McPhee's *Oranges*, he recounts his quest in 1965 to find fresh-squeezed orange juice—his luck, even in the heart of Florida orange country, wasn't good. Every restaurant and welcome station served concentrate, and he finally resorted to picking and squeezing his own. One of the restaurants where he made the request had a grove heavy with oranges just steps away, but it only served concentrate. A couple overhearing his request mentioned that they had a grove of their own, and although they drank concentrate for breakfast each morning, they hadn't made juice from their own trees for more than a decade.

Demand for frozen concentrated orange juice, driven by health-based ads, had also driven advances in the technology of adding back flavor. The old-fashioned days of just adding back non-concentrate orange juice to boost the flavor were over by the 1960s. Orange juice was boiled to high viscosity in a vacuum, and what was added back in instead of just regular-strength juice also included oils, essences and flavor derived from oranges, but separated out as chemical components to be reassembled in exact ratios and frozen so that the flavor for each brand was consistent. As one researcher told McPhee, "We're growing chemicals now, not oranges." They continued to perfect the techniques into what would later be called "flavor packs."

The most important measurement when it comes to orange juice is something called degrees Brix. It's a scale of sugar solution determined by a German scientist of the 1800s named Adolf F.W. Brix. Most orange juice, squeezed directly from an orange, has about 12 degrees Brix, as in, for every one hundred pounds of water there are twelve pounds of sugar.

For frozen concentrate in the 1960s, the process ran thusly—first pulp was removed, then the mixture was heat-evaporated until reaching as high as 70 degrees Brix. By this time, it's less of a liquid and more of a chewy paste. The process robbed the mixture of most of its flavor, but it's at this point that the so-called cutback of regular-strength orange juice and flavorings were added back in, taking it to about 45 degrees Brix, which is then frozen.

A considerable amount of money came from the by-products of juicing, and in the 1960s, about $14 million per year came back to the industry from that alone. Peel oil and components derived from it were (and still are) massively important in the flavor and fragrance industry. Perfume, lotions, candy, cake mixes and even Coca-Cola used it—at the time Coke was one of largest users of peel oil, mainly for the distinctive d-limonene. Other industries also used the leavings of orange juice; a pharmaceutical made from the hesperidin in oranges was used to stop leaks in blood vessels and a powered chemical foam was even derived from the peels to put out forest fires.

More naturally, orange waste in Florida has always been associated with cattle, and there have been orange barons who bought cattle with the idea in mind to feed them the rinds and pulp, such as Ben Hill Griffin Jr., who owned his own concentrate plant, and the Carlton family, who are still in the cattle business here in Florida today. The feed was made by either making a molasses or drying the pulp and chopped rinds for feed.

ANITA BRYANT AND THE GAYCOTT OF FLORIDA ORANGE JUICE

To market juice in the 1960s and '70s, the Florida Citrus Commission needed ads on TV and in magazines, and it wanted more than just pictures of oranges or a family enjoying a healthful morning beverage. What it needed was a face, a spokesperson.

They tapped Anita Bryant, a married Florida dweller who hailed from Oklahoma. With pale skin and dark hair, she'd won Miss Oklahoma at the age of eighteen in 1958 and was a runner-up in the 1959 Miss America Pageant. In the early 1960s, she achieved success as a vocalist, gaining gold records for "Paper Roses," "In My Little Corner of the World" and "'Til There Was You" in the years from 1959 to 1961. She also traveled with the USO, joining Bob Hope and entertaining the troops during the 1960s.

At the age of twenty-seven in 1969, she appeared on TV screens across the nation. In the most iconic ad, she stabbed an orange with a spigot, and fresh Florida orange juice flowed into a glass. An early 1970s TV ad had her wearing a white bell-sleeved dress, caressing an orange on the tree as she sang "Come to the Florida Sunshine Tree."

While Bryant used her wholesome good looks and voice to sell orange juice, she got involved in Christian politics at a time when gay rights activists and advocates called for change. The same year she first appeared as the face and voice of Florida orange juice was also the year of the raid of the New York gay club the Stonewall Inn, when a routine bust of the LGBT community sparked a riot.

Although pro-gay opinions weren't largely popular, laws quietly began to be passed throughout the nation, and by 1977, forty cities and counties, and one state (Pennsylvania), had nondiscrimination laws on the books.

Bryant was horrified when liberals on the Miami–Dade County Commission passed a homosexual nondiscrimination ordinance. The law didn't set precedent, as it followed the same lines as laws written in other jurisdictions, but it was the first time they were called to national attention. She and other members of her church spoke out against the proposed legislation, to no avail.

In response, Bryant created the group Save Our Children, campaigning for voters to veto the homosexual nondiscrimination ordinance with a special referendum, gathering thousands of signatures. With funding and support from the religious right, Save Our Children began its campaign. In a direct mail fundraising letter from Anita Bryant Ministries, she noted, "I don't hate the homosexuals! But as a mother, I must protect my children from their evil

A January Scene–Riding Through Orange Groves in Florida.

Above: Railway lines and the citrus industry were vitally connected, both for tourism and transport. Postcard, 1910. *Author's collection.*

Right: Modern take on the Jesse Fish Cocktail, formulated by Jason Gustavson of Prohibition Kitchen in St. Augustine. *Author's collection.*

Native Americans were often a worry for early settlers, especially during the Seminole Wars. *Department of Defense, U.S. Marine Corps (Photo #306073-A).*

Postcard of Dr. Garnett's Grove. *Souvenir Folder of St. Augustine, Florida, H.&W.B. Drew Company, 18, #22414.*

Citrus label for Mocking Bird, one of the companies in Citra and Florida's State Bird. *Brenda Eubanks Burnette personal collection.*

Satsuma Orange featured on the 1930s *Glen St. Mary Catalogue cover. Glen St. Mary Nursery Collection.*

Left: Pineapple Orange. U.S. Department of Agriculture Pomological Watercolor Collection, Rare and Special Collections, National Agricultural Library, Beltsville, MD, 20705.

Below: The Orange Shop, opened in 1936, still operates in Citra today. *Author's collection.*

Right: Parson Brown. U.S. Department of Agriculture Pomological Watercolor Collection, Rare and Special Collections, National Agricultural Library, Beltsville, MD, 20705.

Below: Foyer of the Howey House. *By Shanejayhayes, Wikimedia Commons.*

Above: Sunsational Citrus's Big Orange. *Author's collection.*

Left: Orange-flavored soft serve ice cream is popular at orange tourist stops. This one is from Sunsational Citrus. *Author's collection.*

Making citrus candy the old-fashioned way, even today, at Davidson of Dundee. *Davidson of Dundee.*

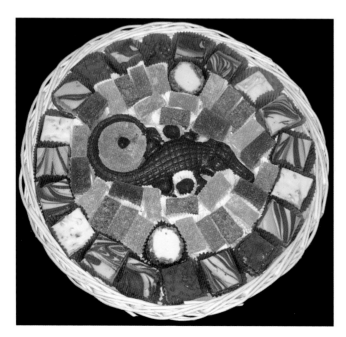

The Fancy Gator Basket from Davidson of Dundee, with a chocolate gator and citrus candies. *Davidson of Dundee.*

A postcard showing pickers at work in an Indian River Orange Grove. 1898. *Detroit Publishing Company collection, Library of Congress.*

Living quarters and "juke joint" for migratory workers, a slack season at Belle Glade. 1944. *Library of Congress, Prints and Photographs Division.*

Above: The hills of Clermont, which would have been visible from the Clermont Citrus Tower, sadly gone after the 1986 freeze. From the 1940s. *Brenda Eubanks Burnette personal collection.*

Left: Temple Orange. 1916. *U.S. Department of Agriculture Pomological Watercolor Collection, Rare and Special Collections, National Agricultural Library, Beltsville, MD, 20705.*

Left: *Lue Gim Gong Orange. U.S. Department of Agriculture Pomological Watercolor Collection, Rare and Special Collections, National Agricultural Library, Beltsville, MD, 20705.*

Below: University of Tampa's Plant Hall was formerly known as the Tampa Bay Hotel, Henry Plant's luxury hotel, opened in 1891. *Author's collection.*

Above: Mural of Lue Gim Gong, no longer standing, which used to be in Deland. *West Volusia Historical Society.*

Right: Bertha Palmer, titled *Mrs. Potter Palmer* (1893), by Anders Zorn, a Swedish portrait painter who painted *Kings and Presidents.*

Left: 1930s citrus label. You can see they were part of two cooperatives, Seald and Lake Wales Citrus Growers. *Brenda Eubanks Burnette personal collection.*

Below: Citrus crate labels (which had their heyday sometime between 1920 and World War II) often featured Native Americans. 1932. *Brenda Eubanks Burnette personal collection.*

Above: Flamingo Groves Label. *Flamingo Gardens Archives, Davie, Florida.*

Left: Paul Meador peels an orange with a pocket knife. *Author's collection.*

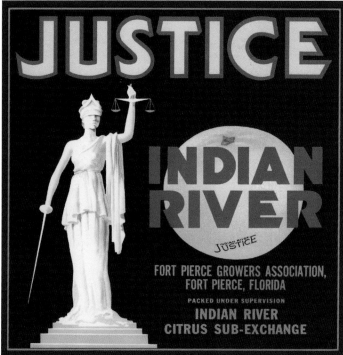

This page and opposite: A wide variety of subject matter can be found on Florida citrus crate labels. A blue background meant the highest quality of Grade A, with red for Grade B and yellow or green for Grade C. Pine companies throughout Florida mainly supplied the wood for the crates, while the printing of the labels was mostly handled in Tampa. *Brenda Eubanks Burnette personal collection.*

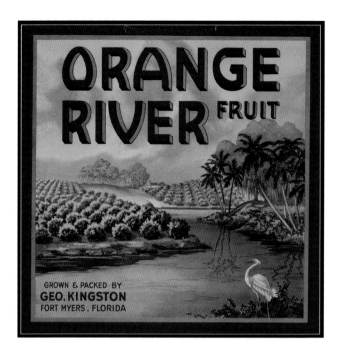

Landscape scenes, especially of water, featured prominently on many labels. *Brenda Eubanks Burnette personal collection.*

Family pets or a particular breed of animal made a citrus brand label memorable. *Brenda Eubanks Burnette personal collection.*

influence....They want to recruit your children and teach them the virtues of becoming a homosexual."

As she was still a spokeswoman for Florida oranges, and most known for that, promoters against the legislation capitalized on the wholesome images of Florida oranges. Save Our Children hired a conservative political consultant to produce a TV ad, comparing Miami's Orange Bowl Parade with the San Francisco Pride Parade. A pretty, all-American girl twirling a baton for the Orange Bowl Parade contrasted with decadent images of the pride parade and of a man in a studded leather halter. Atop the images, a voiceover says, "The Orange Bowl Parade, Miami's gift to the nation, wholesome entertainment. But in San Francisco, when they take to the streets, it's a parade of homosexuals, men hugging other men, cavorting with little boys. The same people who turned San Francisco into a hotbed of homosexuality want to do the same thing to Dade County."

In a 1977 who's-who interview at a local Miami TV station, Bryant said, "According to the word of God it's an abomination...our pastor... would even burn down the school rather than allow them to be taught by homosexuals, and we feel as strongly." In the same segment, Robert Kunst, gay advocate and coauthor of the amendment, said that they welcomed her shining a spotlight on the issue, "The non-gays and the gays are talking for the first time...[there's] absolutely incredible dialogue in every level of this community...every single family is talking about it, and who could have done it but Anita Bryant."

A boycott of Florida orange juice began in gay bars across the nation in 1977. Bars in San Francisco, at the time America's gayest city, posted that they did not serve Florida orange juice in promotion of human rights, and in some places, you could even get a Screwdriver for half-price if you brought your own California oranges, with the bar providing small hand squeezers. Even some of those that catered to straight patrons poured what Florida orange juice they did have already in stock out on the street.

The first openly gay city commissioner in the United States, Harvey Milk, urged readers in his column for the *Bay Area Reporter*, a San Francisco weekly gay newspaper, to switch to pineapple juice for breakfast. Not only did he and local bar owners promote the so-called gaycott of Florida orange juice, but a cottage industry of anti-Anita protest gear also cropped up—buttons that said "Squeeze Anita!," a T-shirt reading "A Day without Human Rights Is Like a Day without Sunshine" under a rough-skinned orange graphic reminiscent of the Death Star and other clever slogans found their way onto wearable protest art.

Bryant's involvement, along with an ad putting the very symbol of Florida wholesomeness front and center, led to protests. The Florida Citrus Commission was inundated with letters against Bryant's stance. Still, public opinion at large supported crushing the legislation, and the amendment was repealed. With that success, Bryant and others began traveling to other places across the country that had passed similar laws, and they were successful in getting some of those repealed.

During a press conference Bryant held about her anti-homosexual views, after the successful repeal of the Dade County law, a gay man pied her, smashing a pie in her face in protest. Her immediate response: "Well, at least it was a fruit pie," a quick quip because gays were known as "fruits" in the 1970s. They did pray for the man who threw the pie afterward. Her husband and manager, Bob Green, found the four gay men who had come to pie Anita in the parking lot afterward, and pied one of them, using a spare banana cream pie they'd brought.

Although gay rights advocates lost the fight, they did succeed in helping to sink her career, souring Bryant's relationship with the Florida Citrus Commission, which didn't want oranges politicized. Not only that, but according to a 1977 article in the *Washington Post*, she also lost the chance to star in her own show, which was to have been sponsored by the Singer Sewing Machines, entitled *The Anita Bryant Show*. The company cited her involvement in "controversial political activities," saying that it wanted the show to be a pleasant experience. Bryant pointed to the refusal as evidence of blacklisting. By 1978, the Florida Citrus Commission had fired her, and she no longer appeared in ads.

In 1980, she divorced her husband, Bob Green. Because by this time her bread and butter came from speaking and singing at fundamentalist churches, that move destroyed what little income she was bringing in. "There were those who said, 'You've written all these books about family togetherness and we're not supporting you anymore. We're not into buying your books and records anymore,'" Green recalled in a *Miami Herald* article.

In an interview with the *Ladies Home Journal* the year of her divorce, she glossed over her former view of homosexuality, saying that "the answers don't seem so simple now." Although she didn't come out in favor of anything so radical as the ERA bill in that interview, she did address the problem of misogyny in the church and conceded that those she had called militant feminists had "valid reasons" to protest.

Bryant remarried in 1990. Over the years since, she experienced various tax problems and bankruptcy, while still occasionally performing to relaunch her career on a local level. Today, she lives in her home state of Oklahoma.

In gay pop culture, her status as an icon has faded, although drag queens occasionally dress up as Anita Bryant. In 2016, Los Angeles's Cavern Club Celebrity debuted the play *Anita Bryant's Playboy Interview*, a staging of Bryant's actual interview with *Playboy* that she gave in 1978. Anita was played by a drag queen.

"NOT FROM CONCENTRATE" AND THE ORANGE JUICE WARS

While frozen concentrate was a craze of the day in the 1950s and '60s, it wasn't the only orange juice product on the market. Tropicana in particular was the biggest name in the chilled juice business. Its process involved heating up the orange juice to about two hundred degrees in flash pasteurization, to kill the enzymes, keeping the solids from settling too much. During the winter, it froze the surplus regular-strength juice into huge blocks, which, come summer time, it would crack up, feed into an ice crusher and melt down. This differed from other chilled juice suppliers at the time, which reconstituted concentrate instead and put it on the shelves at regular strength.

Tropicana mostly sourced from Florida in those days, but in 1962 a freeze came, cutting the Florida orange crop by one-third. It had customers, but not enough fruit to supply them, so it put the processing equipment on a ship, anchored off the coast of Mexico and bought Mexican oranges at a cheap price. Since everyone else was having problems with supply at the time, it gained profits and introduced Mexican-sourced orange juice to the United States. But the Mexican government soon raised the price of oranges, and Tropicana sold the ship and equipment for a loss of $2 million.

Finding that cartons let in too much oxygen, the company decided to make its own glass bottles in 1964, and in 1968, it became the first citrus industry company to operate its own plastic container manufacturing plant.

The rivalry between juice companies to capture as many brand-loyal drinkers as possible, known as the "Orange Juice Wars," didn't really heat up until the 1980s, but there were clashes in the 1970s, primarily between Minute Maid (owned by Coca-Cola) and Tropicana.

Tropicana wasn't yet a national brand, although it had been expanding. The king of concentrate, Minute Maid, was nervous about the changes in the market—chilled orange juice now accounted for 31 percent of the orange market, a 10 percent bump in status from the late 1960s just a few years earlier. In 1973, Minute Maid began an incursion into metropolitan New York with its chilled juice, an area that had been firmly in Tropicana's hands.

The debate over the superiority of Tropicana's never-from-concentrate chilled juice versus Minute Maid's reconstituted from-concentrate chilled juice had begun. Tropicana maintained that its product was the more natural of the two because it came direct from an orange—after pasteurization, of course—but Minute Maid contended that concentration gave it the ability to blend juices from different varieties of oranges, controlling the flavor for a consistent product. Minute Maid, which already had a national supply chain set up because of frozen concentrate, became the first national chilled orange juice brand. Tropicana shot back at Minute Maid as best it could in 1975 by entering the frozen concentrate biz.

As far as a consistent product is concerned, at least in the early days, Minute Maid wasn't wrong. The flavor and sweetness of a fresh-squeezed orange has immense variation depending on when you pick them, what type they are, even where on the tree they grew. Fruit on higher branches are sweeter, as are the fruit grown on the outside rather than the inner branches. Oranges grown on the north side of a tree are less sweet than those grown in any other side of the tree. Even within a single orange, each segment can contain a variation of vitamin C, flavor and sweetness.

By the 1980s, Tropicana did have a consistent product, making full use of scientific measurement, blending juices of varying Brix and adding flavors derived from orange juice to its not-from-concentrate juice.

The top three brands in the 1980s were Minute Maid, Procter & Gamble's Citrus Hill Brand and Tropicana. Tropicana offered different products— frozen concentrate and a cheaper from-concentrate brand alongside its unique not-from-concentrate product. While Citrus Hill and Minute Maid offered a variety as well, when it came to chilled juice, both were still selling from-concentrate products at the start of the '80s.

The year 1983 brought a freeze to Florida, and Tropicana had to raise its prices several times over the season. It was shocked to find that there wasn't a drop in the amount consumers purchased. Customers were willing to pay for what they saw as a superior product, so with the profits Tropicana began heavily marketing its juice as not-from-concentrate, beginning the Orange Juice Wars as the three top brands fought for the top market share, a fight that would continue through the 1990s.

Having lost the argument in the marketplace as to the superiority of from-concentrate, Minute Maid finally introduced its own not-from-concentrate chilled orange juice in 1988. But it included the phrase "straight from the orange" in its advertisements, and Tropicana sued over it. Minute Maid opted to drop the slogan rather than battle it out in court. By 1990, Minute Maid had 11.7 percent of the non-concentrate market, but Tropicana managed to outperform Minute Maid in the overall juice market by just 0.1 percent—22.3 percent to Minute Maid's 22.2 percent. Considering the juggernaut status of Minute Maid, even a tenth of a percent was a massive victory. Citrus Hill fared worse and worse as the top two contenders battled, and in 1992, Procter & Gamble discontinued the Citrus Hill line.

Both Minute Maid and Tropicana scrambled to fill the void Citrus Hill had left. Tropicana won out in the early 1990s, capturing a wider lead in the overall market in 1993 with 30.1 percent to Minute Maid's 25.9 percent. In the later 1990s, Tropicana continued to grow, this time on an international scale.

Minute Maid survived the Orange Juice Wars, but it hadn't come away unscathed. Coca-Cola Foods, the division of the company Minute Maid was under, was the only division of the company to have claimed a loss in 1995. Tropicana claimed even more of the market share in 1996, with 32.4 percent to Minute Maid's 24.3 percent. Later that year, Minute Maid opted to drop its non-concentrate chilled juice in favor of rejuvenating its from-concentrate chilled juice and frozen concentrate. It also began expanding internationally, returning to profitability in 1997.

Tropicana, whose parent company had changed multiple times over the years, was sold to PepsiCo in 1998, which owns the company today.

Today, Tropicana, Minute Maid and Florida's Natural together account for 66 percent of the overall orange juice market and 80 percent of the not-from-concentrate juice market.

CRITICISM IN THE 2000s

In the 2009 book *Squeezed: What You Don't Know About Orange Juice* by Alissa Hamilton, the reality of the industry processes came out, revealing the orange industry to be perhaps less close to nature than its marketing might suggest. It's been hurtful to the juice industry, which has worked hard to make a consistent product from oranges available year round. There have been hundreds of articles since, both in print and online, that have asked the question: "Is orange juice healthy?"

Tropicana's quaint practice of freezing its single-strength juice for storage had been left behind in the wake of the Orange Juice Wars. The practice adopted by most juice-makers, and the one used today, is to de-oxygenate the orange juice completely, storing in anaerobic tanks for up to a year, a process that, like the concentrate process of old, completely strips away anything enjoyable about drinking it.

Flavor is added back using flavor packs, many derived from the oranges themselves, though not always. For the public, learning that something such as ethyl butyrate is added to enhance flavor sounds terrifying and unnatural—but it is something you'd be eating if you bit into an apple or ate a pineapple, though perhaps not in high quantities.

Besides criticisms leveled at orange juice regarding storage practices and so-called natural flavors, the amount of sugar in a glass of OJ has also been called to the public's attention. Articles such as *Huffington Post's* "Is Juice Really Worse than Soda?" point out that juice has about the same amount of sugar as a soda (roughly five to eight teaspoons per cup), ending the article by calling a moratorium on both beverages in favor of brewing up some green tea or steeping orange slices in water.

It takes about two to four oranges to make one cup, or eight ounces of orange juice. And it is sweet. That's why we like it. Growers definitely used the healthy image to gain an edge on their competition, while having enough sugar to stand up to the lure of soda drinks, but we can at least say that orange juice is a source of vitamin C.

Something like flavor packs may or may not matter to you, but if they do, there are guides online denoting which companies use them and which don't. If you want as natural as possible, buy whole oranges and squeeze them yourself. But if you want convenience and a taste of Florida, you'll probably buy orange juice from the store. There are a lot more choices when it comes to juice, as far as process is concerned, with lots of niche brands.

Many companies use blends from other countries (which might be less regulated and might contain pesticides banned in the United States). You can look for brands like Florida's Natural if you want juice that's exclusively Floridian and American. Haines City, home of the first citrus juicing plant in 1915, is currently the headquarters to a cooperative of citrus farmers with 170 members and about 9,000 acres within 120 miles of Haines City. The cooperative offers grove management, harvesting, marketing and fresh fruit packing. It's part of Florida's Natural Growers, so any surplus it has goes to juice. The organization was founded back in 1909 with six local growers, making it one of the oldest co-ops in the state. Today, it has a packinghouse facility located on its original 7.5 acres in downtown Haines City.

Worldwide, Florida is the second-largest producer of orange juice (behind Brazil), with more than seventy-five thousand Floridians working in the citrus or a related business, garnering more than $8.6 billion in economic activity.

FIGURES AND HISTORY OF THE WEST COAST

The West Coast of Florida has its own culture and connection to oranges. In the past two centuries, the populace of the West Coast made their money in much the same way as the rest of Florida, through agriculture, timber and oranges. But the people of Tampa Bay also made their dollars diving for sponges, smuggling on the water, running billiard halls, soldiering at Fort Brooke and rolling cigars.

Tampa Bay served as a shipping point for fruit, vegetables and other goods, by ship and by railway, both from the surrounding counties and Central Florida. While the Flagler railroad snaked its way down the east coast of the state, Henry Plant claimed the west coast in the late 1800s, and it was the Plant railway that connected Tampa by land to the rest of Florida.

In the 1880s, Tampa was headquarters to the Orange Growers Convention, and about thirty years after the inaugural year of the convention, the Florida Citrus Exchange was founded in 1909 out of that convention. The Florida Citrus Exchange, later to become Seald Sweet Growers, was a huge influence on citrus in Florida.

Citrus cooperatives such as Seald Sweet have been mentioned throughout this book, and they have been crucial to the development of the orange industry. Cooperatives can serve all kinds of purposes—driving prices down for fertilizer and fungicide by collective buying, sending representatives to find new markets (some of which might only be available if a high volume can be supplied), setting standards for a geographic area, giving out short-term loans on the basis of a member's projected crops and even providing security to the groves to prevent fruit theft.

It's no coincidence that many of the local Florida co-ops were formed or gathered much more membership in late '20s and early '30s, when there was a glut of fruit on the market and no one to buy it. In this era, Seald Sweet pushed the idea of cooperatives as the best way to do business. As a statewide co-op itself, it encouraged membership from within the local co-op groups, while allowing those local organizations their idiosyncrasies.

The main aim of Seald, although it helped in many different areas, was marketing Florida citrus on a global scale. Its monthly newspaper, the *Seald Sweet Chronicle*, featured many articles and authoritative quotes from farmers, the secretary of agriculture and even Calvin Coolidge—whose words were featured in bold boxes alongside the informational articles: "More than anything else we need a generation of farmers trained to cooperative marketing."

The paper also presented the other side of the argument (although it was clear what side it was on)—that cooperatives smacked of Communism and that ad buys and marketing were a waste of money because the increasing chain stores across the country only cared about low price, not colorful billboards and newspaper ads. Still, Seald's ads were strongly a part of the national consciousness for more than fifty years, and although today it isn't the powerhouse it became through the 1960s, Seald Sweet still exists in 2019.

EARLY DAYS

One of the earliest Europeans to settle in the Tampa Bay area, the fabled Odet Philippe, had quite an impact on citrus in the state. He's also one of the few people of color in this early era to own and propagate groves. He's listed as originally being a French citizen in paperwork, but it was possible he never saw France and instead hailed from the French West Indies—a part of the Caribbean colonized by France.

There are records of Philippe living in different areas of Florida before starting business dealings in Tampa Bay beginning in the late 1830s, including Key West and in a part of Monroe County that would later become sectioned off as Dade County. He arrived in the New River area in about 1828–29. The Cooley Massacre in 1836 spooked Philippe, and like many New River residents, he left for Key West afterward. Native Americans reportedly attacked the Cooley Plantation, near Philippe's land, killing most of the family there, including a baby. As the U.S. government was looking for people to settle Tampa Bay, and it was near enough Fort Brooke for security, Philippe also bought land there.

He's become something of a legend in Tampa Bay, because much of what is known about him is apocryphal. For one thing, there's a tale of a probably untrue connection with Napoleon. Phillipe was too young to have been Napoleon's contemporary. We know that he admired Napoleon Bonaparte because he named his plantation St. Helena, after the island where Napoleon banished and buried. He also named his ship the *Ney*, after one of the more celebrated marshals of Napoleon's army.

Philippe was called a count, although he probably wasn't officially a real count, and sometimes passed himself off as a doctor. He was rumored to be the head surgeon of Napoleon's army, also pretty likely a fiction. As doctors were in short supply in many of the places he lived, patients valued anyone with some experience, even if they hadn't had schooling. The story that he briefly served as a physician on a pirate ship after the *Ney* was captured is certainly possible, if a bit far-fetched.

By the time he came to Tampa, he was a wealthy man, but as to how he earned that wealth, it remains murky, although there is speculation that he might have made his money through the slave trade or pirate dealings during his time in Key West. Historian and Odet Philippe descendant J. Allison DeFoor II noted that Philippe made money through connections in Charleston and Key West, as well as probably the illegal slave trade.

Once in Tampa Bay, Odet Philippe established his plantation, St. Helena, where he planted citrus. Agriculturally, he's most famous for being the pioneer of grapefruit, but he also planted bananas, limes, avocados, pears and oranges, which he acquired earlier in the Caribbean.

His propagation of citrus in these early days helped spread of citrus all over Florida, as well as more locally in Hillsborough and Pinellas Counties. With his neighbors he shared budwood as well as tips and tricks on how to bud sour orange trees with sweet oranges.

Although a hurricane temporarily destroyed his plantation in 1848, an old Indian mound served as refuge for Philippe's family, and he rebuilt and replanted afterward. Besides being credited with bringing the cigar making industry to Tampa, he also ran a billiard hall, traded in livestock and engaged in land speculation and the slave trade. He left the plantation during the Civil War, residing in Pasco County instead for the duration. He came back to St. Helena after the war, dying on his plantation in 1869.

Today you can visit the site of the St. Helena Plantation at Philippe Park in Pinellas County. Although the plantation house and groves are no more, the mound still stands, as does a commemorative plaque.

THE LATE 1800s

The connection of the Plant railway system was a boon to all the industries in the area, including agriculture, but unlike most anticipated railway builds, it didn't touch off land sales prior to the build because no one believed Plant would complete it. In 1883, the charter to build the railway from Sanford to Tampa belonged to Alfred H. Parslow, but Parslow didn't have enough money to do the build, and he was running out of time because the rights to the federal land grant would end in January 1884. Before it did, he sold the rights to Henry Plant in June 1883. Everyone thought that Plant was crazy to try, but on January 23, just two days before the deadline, the lines met.

While Flagler's involvement developed the east coast of Florida, Plant's railway and the hotels he opened (especially in Tampa Bay) helped to put the city of Tampa in the public consciousness and as a destination. Henry Plant's luxury hotels and social events brought moneyed individuals to the west coast, leading to development. John Jacob Astor even brought his wife to one of Plant's hotels for their honeymoon.

University of Tampa's Plant Hall was formerly known as the Tampa Bay Hotel—Henry Plant's luxury hotel, opened in 1891. *Author's collection.*

One of the benchmarks for the development of Tampa Bay, besides the formation of the Plant railway system, was the Spanish-American War in 1898. So many soldiers came to the Tampa area that the infrastructure couldn't handle it, and some were garrisoned in more central counties. Nevertheless, the thousands of soldiers sent through Florida on their way to support a free Cuba garnered two things: a captive audience to see the area and its opportunities firsthand and the spotlight of the press on Florida, in particular Tampa Bay. Those two factors laid a foundation for the further development of Tampa, including the citrus industry.

The 1894–95 freezes killed orange trees here, just like nearly every other area in Florida—snow even fell in Hillsborough County. A severe storm also hit the Tampa area in September 1896, so any trees that did survive the carnage of the freeze were either stripped of fruit and leaf or killed. In the last five years of the 1800s, the population of orange growers changed because of these disasters, but all in all, there was a net gain of citrus growers by the early 1900s. Farmers in more northerly counties came down to try their luck in Hillsborough, some left Tampa Bay or grew a different crop or tried a different business and a few stalwart souls with enough capital to burn replanted.

In a promotional real estate pamphlet published in July 1896, the major industries were sponge collection, timber, cattle and agriculture. Among the things grown were alligator pears, guava, mango, sugar apple, plums, coffee plant, grapes and pineapple. The pamphlet claimed citrus as a chief crop, especially around Dunedin.

BUCKEYE NURSERY AND THE TEMPLE ORANGE

The origins of the Temple orange in Florida are cloudy at best, with connections all over the state. We do know that it was named after William Chase Temple, an influential grower who was the first president of the Florida Citrus Exchange.

A fellow named D.C. Gillette out of Buckeye Nursery in Tampa popularized it. There's more than one story as to how he got his hands on the budwood (some say his father brought the Jamaican orange to Florida). A personal account from Ethel Hakes in the *Florida Grower*, as to how her husband, Louis Hakes, "discovered" the tree growing in their groves, is probably fairly accurate.

She acknowledges that what we now call the Temple was likely from Jamaica, and she believes it was probably introduced to Florida prior to

1894. When Louis tried one of the oranges from the tree in their Winter Park grove, he knew they had something special and asked the advice of William Chase Temple, who confirmed the excellence of the orange, connecting the Hakeses with Buckeye's D.C. Gillette.

The taste of Temple is tart and complex, and it's thought to be not a pure orange, but a hybrid—a tangor, a cross between a tangerine and an orange. It's one of the best eating oranges out there, but today it's not always easy to find, although it can be ordered in gift baskets during the season.

Gillette suggested they name the orange and then patent it, selling it exclusively through Buckeye, requiring every grower who bought the budwood not to sell or give it away. The *Florida Grower*'s editorial suggestion that they name the orange after William Chase Temple, an important figure in citrus on top of being the intermediary and advice-giver regarding the orange, was taken to heart by Gillette and the Hakeses.

Once the patent went through, no grower could sell oranges under the name Temple unless those oranges had come from budwood sold by Buckeye Nurseries.

The relatives of the African American grower Price Butler Boston of Oviedo claim that he was the first to grow the orange in Florida, but he didn't get a patent. According to the family, the orange spread to numerous groves in Florida and eventually was noticed by Louis Hakes and patented by Buckeye, some twenty years after Boston introduced it.

World War I put a stop to putting the budwood into major propagation, as they thought there would be little demand for it, but once the war ended in 1919, Buckeye Nursery couldn't fill orders fast enough.

The oranges were central to building a community just outside of Tampa, Temple Terrace. Chicago socialite Bertha Palmer, a wealthy landowner and patron of the arts, had a dream to develop the land into a golf course community. The capable Palmer had helped Sarasota blossom into the "City of the Arts" that it is today.

Unfortunately, she died in 1918 before she could realize her golf-community vision, but her brother, Adrian Honoré, found a group of men who wanted to go forward with it. One of them was D.C. Gillette. Two corporations were founded by Gillette and his partners: Temple Terrace Estates Inc., which encompassed the golf course and residential areas, and Temple Terraces Inc., which budded five thousand acres of Temple oranges, surrounding the city to the west and north. It was probably one of the largest groves in the state at the time (quickly outstripped by others, such as Dr. Phillips's gigantic grove in Orange County, more than twice that size). To attract buyers, the community allowed house owners to buy in shares of the grove, and the profits could then offset the cost of buying property and homes there.

Although there are orange trees in the yards of some of the houses in Temple Terrace, they are not from the original stock. You will find a historic marker proclaiming the area the site of the "World's Largest Orange Grove" at the corner of Gillette Avenue and East 113th Avenue, next to the Greco Middle School track in Temple Terrace.

THE TWENTIETH CENTURY THROUGH 2000

One of the most notable figures in the early part of the 1900s was John S. Taylor, born in the Largo area of Pinellas County in 1871. His parents were pioneers who owned an orange grove and packinghouse. Taylor built on that foundation with a packinghouse of his own, finished in 1902. It became central to the economy in the area.

Politically, Taylor was a mover and a shaker, campaigning to form Pinellas County as we know it by 1912. He served as a representative of Hillsborough County before it became Pinellas in 1905–10 and then as the chair of the Pinellas County Board of Commissioners from 1915 to 1923. He also became a Florida state senator, eventually becoming the president of the Florida Senate. While there, he promoted citrus interests and legislation. He was also known because he opposed teaching evolution in Florida schools, supporting a bill to ban teaching the theory in schools in 1927. The bill did not pass, and the following year, he unsuccessfully ran for governor.

During the Great Depression, Taylor's groves and packing plant were a bulwark against the worsening economy. Not just active in politics, he also garnered the title of president of the Bank of Clearwater and steward of Largo Methodist Church, and just one year before his death, he became president of the Florida Citrus Exchange in 1935.

From the late 1930s through the 1950s, one of the largest influences in the world of citrus near to Tampa was a man named Ralph Burdick Polk. He had moved his canning concern, Polk Canning, from Haines City to Tampa in the late 1930s. He'd already co-invented the first commercial juice extractor with his son, Ralph Polk Jr. The father-and-son team would hold more than one patent, also holding one for extracting the citrus cells from the inedible portions of the fruit. The improvements he and his son engineered made them pioneers in canning, and Polk Sr. served as an early director of the National Canners Association and was one of the founders of the Florida Canners Association. Like many Florida magnates of the day, he built a hotel, which stands today as the Landmark Baptist College.

Another prominent figure in citrus, whose impact is still present today, is Dr. Karl Benjamin Albritton. Born in 1900, his family came to Sarasota after their Polk County citrus groves died in a bad freeze. In the 1920s, although he never graduated from high school, he studied agriculture and was one of the people who helped with the eradication of the Mediterranean fruit fly outbreak of the 1930s. Throughout his life, he worked with Citrus Research and Education Center in Lake Alfred, sharing research and data with it. He was also involved with a number of organizations: Citrus Growers Inc. (later the Florida Farm Bureau), 4-H and Future Farmers of America. Among his other achievements, he also designed one of the first citrus hedgers in the state, although he never got a patent. His achievements earned him a place not just in the Florida Citrus Hall of Fame but also in the Florida Agriculture Hall of Fame.

The year 1947 saw the opening of his packinghouse, Albritton Fruit Company. He was one of the first in the state to open shops to sell local agricultural products such as honey and fruit, eventually opening up several stores in Port Charlotte, Sarasota, Venice and Englewood. His family company grew, picked, processed, juiced and sold oranges directly to the public, feeding rinds to their cattle concern. By the mid-1990s, during the citrus season, it employed two hundred people, and of that two hundred, fifty were year-round employees.

Dr. Karl Benjamin Albritton died at the age of 101 in 2002, but his legacy lives on. You can still visit the Albritton Fruit Company during the season in the city of Sarasota.

LATE 1990s TO TODAY

As of the 2016–17 season, Hillsborough had just 3,431 acres devoted to oranges. It's the best of the west coast batch of counties from Cedar Key to Sarasota. Total commercial acres of oranges for each of the other counties are as follows: Hernando, 472; Pasco, 1,751; Sarasota, 867; and none for Levy and Pinellas Counties.

In 1998, a little under nineteen years before the 2016–17 season, orange acreage was at 25,113 for Hillsborough, 10,507 for Pasco, 987 for Hernando and 1,699 for Sarasota County. Levy was still at zero, but in the late 1990s,

Pinellas was just hanging on with 104 acres. There's been a significant drop in these counties for citrus acreage overall, attributable to the various pests and diseases that have plagued the industry, from citrus canker to the more recent citrus greening.

In Pasco County, near the city of Odessa, Cee Bee's Citrus Emporium closed in 2018. The family-run business couldn't cope with all the trials related to citrus. Scientists in the state are beginning to understand how to manage citrus greening, but over the years, it's devastated their crops enough that they couldn't recover. The arrival of Hurricane Irma in 2017 knocked off most of what they did have.

DUNEDIN ORANGE FESTIVAL AND TOURIST STOPS

Dunedin's orange history reaches as far back as the 1880s, but it really saw its height during World War II, when the city was shipping out concentrate for British and American troops. After a factory fire in the 1950s, the industry has slowly lessened over the years, with the land given over to cattle and real estate.

In April 2009, artist Steve Spathelf and local resident Marsha Goins secretly painted images of oranges on buildings in downtown Dunedin

Florida Orange Groves Winery. Retail locations are spread throughout Florida, but the main store is located in St. Petersburg. *Author's collection.*

at 5:00 a.m. Spathelf admired and collected the old orange crate labels, particularly local ones from the Skinner and Douglas families, and he was sad to see the old citrus heritage of Dunedin slipping away. Spathelf and Goins's "guerrilla" art garnered quite the response from the community and beyond, as people from all over came to the small city to see the artwork. Local merchants and city leaders seized the opportunity, and in 2010, they held the first Dunedin Orange Festival. It's a small affair at Edgewater Park downtown, and it's held each July, meant to boost business in the slow season and the heat of summer, generally long after the late oranges are off the trees, so you're unlikely to see any fresh, whole Florida oranges while you're there. They have a Dunedin Orange Festival Pin Up Girl Contest, an orange-themed bonnet auction for charity, live music and, of course, free orange juice.

Other options for the west coast orange tourist are, of course, U-Picks and farm stores such as Dooley Farms in the west coast region of Florida today, but one of the more unusual stops in the state is the flagship store for Florida Orange Groves Winery, which sells fruit wines made from Florida fruits, including its Orange Sunshine Wines (comes in dry and sweet) made from 100 percent Florida orange juice.

LEGENDARY ORANGES OF
CENTRAL EAST FLORIDA

The freeze of 1835 might not have made its mark on citrus history as much as the 1894–95 freeze, but all evidence suggests that this freeze was much colder. The salt water of the bays in St. Augustine even froze, and the temperatures plummeted to as low as eleven degrees. Although it killed most of the oranges growing in Florida, because of the hundreds of years of orange growing, it was seen as a fluke, and growers weren't deterred.

Freezes in Florida are like snowflakes, even if none fall from the sky. Each is different, and they vary from area to area. One freeze might strike low-lying areas, and others might hit high ridges when there are winds. A difference of a single degree could save or damn a tree. After every freeze there are so-called miracle groves, somehow spared from the carnage. In the early days, it was hard to understand why, so these groves became legendary. One such grove could be found in the Indian River region.

Douglas Dummett's grove, planted in 1830, was the miracle grove of the 1835 freeze. Using wild sour orange trees as the rootstock, budded with sweet oranges, he'd situated his grove on Merritt Island, with the warm tidal waters of the Banana River on one side and the Indian River on the other; it was also on a high embankment. Dummett's grove on Merritt Island would today be considered in Brevard County. While many trees froze solid and died in 1835, Dummett's grove not only survived but also still had oranges.

Thus began the legend of the Indian River Orange, which eventually proved to be so pervasive that regulation had to be passed to keep orange growers from other portions of the state from labeling their oranges as Indian River Oranges. Even those growing oranges inland, on the Ridge, slapped labels on their orange crate proclaiming them "Indian River Oranges," until regulation stopped them when the Federal Trade Commission issued a cease-and-desist in the 1930s.

Dummett's oranges probably saved the industry—or at the very least made the way easier for the industry to flower after the Civil War. Many Florida oranges grown from 1836 to 1860 reportedly had their origin in buddings from Dummett's oranges. The grove also survived the 1895 freeze.

THE INDIAN RIVER REGION

The Dummett grove survival may have kickstarted the legend, but over the years, this reputation has proven true—Indian River oranges have been a bit more likely to survive a freeze, as well as produce oranges with what many say is a better flavor, perhaps because the soil is slightly richer than in most of Florida but still sandy enough to provide the drainage oranges crave. The soils are underlain by coquina limestone and a shallow water table. The area gets a good fifty-two inches per year on average, as opposed to more inland Central Florida—Polk County gets only thirty-nine inches per year. All citrus, even in moist Florida, needs irrigation, but Indian River growers maintain that natural rain has crucial micro-elements making their fruit better than others in the state.

The official bounds of the Indian River area, as established in 1941, start about ten miles north of Daytona Beach, running down the coast almost to West Palm Beach. From the coastside inland, the strip was about fifteen miles wide, getting a little wider at the southern edge.

The Indian River region, besides having a stellar reputation regarding quality, also had something that parts of Florida at this latitude didn't have: built-in freeze protection. It's why, even in the deepest of freezes, at least some citrus survived, bountiful when other places in the state suffered damage. Most importantly, the region sits close to the Gulf Stream, closer than other parts of the state, even at the same longitude. Take a look at a map of Florida—at Jacksonville Beach, for instance, on the east coast, but farther north than Vero Beach, an east coast city within the Indian River District. Both are on the east edge of the state, but Florida flares out more than you would think, so Vero is actually one hundred miles farther east and is therefore closer to the warmth of the Gulf Stream.

The second factor protecting the region are all the bits of water—lakes, swamps and rivers—that buffer cold fronts. Any fronts coming north to south or west to east have to move past that Central Florida gauntlet of waters.

Lastly, Indian River growers had a trick they used during a freeze allowed by their specific geography. It's a flat region, and they built their groves to flood. Normally, you wouldn't want orange trees with wet roots, but if a freeze was coming, they could pump in warm water as a temporary lake in the groves, a technique that raises temperature during the course of a night between two and four degrees, another defense against freeze damage.

DELAND, FLORIDA

If you lived in New York City, Philadelphia or Chicago in the 1880s and were a regular reader of news, chances were you'd seen one of Henry Addison Deland's ads or stories about Deland, Florida. Deland's daughter, Helen, wrote that "old letters and bills show that he was advertising in about ninety papers and magazines...he asked visiting friends on their return to write articles in their home papers." Henry Deland had orange lands and plenty of them to sell, and more than that, he guaranteed to back your purchase. As sunny as the 1880s orange fever promotional articles and pamphlets were, news had reached the northern states about a series of little freezes in the 1800s, as well as a particularly hard freeze in 1886. Until the 1894–95 freezes, that 1886 freeze was the harshest the orange growers of that generation had seen. For the savvy businessman looking for a flaw in something that seemed too good to be true, the news of these freezes put a bit of a damper on orange fever, and more cautious investors shied away. Deland hoped that his promise of backing would be enough to bring good men to his county and the city named after him.

According to Deland's daughter, the freezes of 1894–95 broke Henry Deland financially, as he sought to pay back those groves he'd guaranteed, "but his spirit was invincible." Like the community of Deland, he started over. In the late 1920s, Helen Deland reported, "The average yearly orange crop of...[Volusia] county runs now well over a million boxes, of which a goodly portion are sent out from Deland."

Picture of pickers sometime in the first half of the twentieth century. *West Volusia Historical Society.*

THE LUE GIM GONG ORANGE

In the late 1880s, Deland's guarantee attracted Major William Dumville and his family. With them came a Chinese man to help manage their groves. The only Chinese person in Deland at the time, Lue Gim Gong seemed an unlikely individual to affect agriculture on a national scale, but before the end of his life, he would.

Born in China in 1860, Lue Gim Gong immigrated to the United States by way of California when he was barely a teenager, just twelve or thirteen. Before he moved to America, his life had been spent in rural Canton, learning agrarian ways in his daily life. In particular, his mother taught him the delicate art of hand pollination. Hearing stories about exotic America from a successful uncle who had immigrated, Lue was attracted by stories of schooling for all and begged to go. His uncle paid for his passage over.

His first job in the States was at a shoe factory in California, and once he gained experience, he found a higher-paying gig of the same kind at the C.T. Sampson Shoe Factory in North Adams, Massachusetts, complete with passage. Like most of the workers hired, he was unaware that he was there to break a strike. It was this job that eventually led him to Florida, albeit in a circuitous manner.

Church leaders in North Adams organized a Sunday school for the workers. The aim of the school was to convert the heathens, since none of the Chinese workers had heard of Jesus. Lue jumped at the chance to come, as it was the first time since he'd come to America that he'd been able to go to a school. The Sunday school taught the pupils English first—after all, it's hard to spread the word of God when the people you're speaking to don't understand a word you're saying.

The Sunday school volunteer teacher, Fanny Amelia Burlingame, took an interest in eager and bookish Lue, eventually tutoring him privately. Although they weren't free from prejudice, Fanny's family had markedly less than most toward Chinese because of their connections to China. Fanny was related to Anson Burlingame, an ambassador to China who negotiated a major trade bill bearing the family name in 1868, which allowed travel between the United States and China.

The kindness and generosity of the Burlingame family, along with time in church, won Lue's loyalty. From this point on, he was devoted to the ideals of Christ, although he still adhered to the philosophy of Confucianism.

In the Burlingame hothouse, he began to experiment with cross-pollination and making up his own blend of non-toxic insect repellent. In the mid-1870s, an economic downturn cut his factory hours, so the boy began living at the Burlingame home, serving as houseboy and gardener and even taking care of Fanny's father after he suffered a stroke.

By 1886, Lue had contracted tuberculosis. Lue went home to China expecting to die but was unexpectedly cured. He had changed greatly since coming to America. His talk of Christianity and science, along with his non-traditional hairstyle (he'd cut off his long queue in favor of short hair) led to him being shunned. He tended his mother's orange groves, but China was no longer home for him. He wrote his "Mother Fanny" and got passage back to the States. Meanwhile, his natural mother arranged his marriage, but Lue was long gone to Deland, Florida, and he never went through with the ceremony, something that his Chinese family never forgave him for.

Lue came to Deland because Fanny's sister's husband had bought an orange grove. Many of the moneyed individuals out of North Adams, Massachusetts, were building vacation homes there, and once the family became familiar with the area, the lure of this profitable crop was not only lucrative but also fashionable. Cynthia Burlingame Dumville; her sister, Fanny; and Cynthia's husband, Major William Dumville, made up the household. Lue could not live in the Deland house because of the community's judgment; he was relegated to a shack on the property, although Lue still ate his meals with Fanny. Lue and the family lived there during the winters and the cooler seasons, escaping the oppressive Florida summers by going back to Massachusetts.

At the time, Lue was the only Chinese person in Deland, and so he did not have any social circle outside the Burlingames and Dumvilles, but he loved to work the earth and believed in America as an idea. In 1887, Fanny secured U.S. citizenship for Lue.

When it came to farming, the observant Lue voraciously collected all the information he could. And he'd seen something no one else had. Winter was coming, and it was going to be deadly to the groves. His theory was that the clear-cutting of the tall pine forests of North Florida and development was changing the weather patterns. He thought that harder freezes, and for longer, were going to be the norm. While most everyone in the late 1880s and early '90s clung fast to the hope that warm weather would last forever, that the little freezes of 1881 and 1886 were just flukes, he was busy cultivating a cold-hardy orange. Lue found that his cross-bred seedlings survived the Big Freezes of 1894 and 1895.

But it wasn't just oranges that Lue developed. His seeds were sold, with Fanny's help, in catalogues across the country—late-ripening peaches, clustering tomatoes and giant grapefruits were among his creations.

It was his winter-hardy orange that he became most known for, thought to be a cross-pollinated "Hart's Late" Valencia orange with a "Mediterranean Sweet," for which he was awarded the Silver Wilder Medal by the American Pomological Society in 1911. Testing later revealed that the "hybrid" was actually a nucellar seedling of "Valencia," which was then propagated and distributed by Glen St. Mary Nurseries in 1912. In any case, Gong had developed a genetically stable, cold-hardy variety of Valencia. So while you might not be able to find an orange specifically marketed as Lue Gim Gong these days, the modern Valencia is fairly close.

Helen Deland, daughter of the founder of Deland, described the virtues of the Lue Gim Gong orange in an exaggerated fashion: "[F]ruit will hang on the tree three years or longer without deterioration.…[It] stands temperatures ten degrees colder than those of other kinds." For the growers left in the state after the Big Freeze, these summer oranges were a godsend, and they were one of the factors that helped the industry rebuild afterward.

The very "Chineseness" that marked him separate from the community was also used by Fanny and others, like the Glen St. Mary Nursery, to market him as a mystical "Citrus Wizard," as though the Lue Gim Gong orange had sprung whole from an ancient Chinese secret. His seedlings and seeds were found in gardens and groves across the nation.

To say that Lue Gim Gong was dependent on Fanny would be an understatement. But his relationship with the family had advantages on both sides. Lue never took wages from the family, despite tending their groves and doing whatever else that was needed. While he was a genius in the grove and garden, finances weren't his bailiwick. Self-interest and profit were things that Lue was never good at, much to his detriment later on. Still, there was one thing he knew he needed: land. So, when Fanny died in 1903, he implored her sisters to deed him the land his shack stood on as well as the acreage of the groves. Since it wasn't of any use to them any longer, they deeded it to him. It would have been what Fanny wanted after all, since on paperwork she'd named him as an adopted son. They also gave him a large sum of $12,000 for back wages over his decades of service to the family.

He bought more land with some of the money. Unfortunately, locals didn't like the idea of a wealthy Chinese, so when harvest time came, he didn't have enough help, as influential city residents discouraged laborers from working with him. He turned to a Swedish immigrant family for help. He eventually asked for their daughter's hand in marriage, but they did not like the idea of a mixed-race marriage and refused him. He would remain single for the rest of his life.

Lue had his eccentricities—he often carried his rooster around the grove, his two horses followed him around like dogs and as he was not welcomed in church because of his race, he made his own outdoor "cathedral." But he was more than happy to talk to anyone about oranges or agriculture and give away buds to anyone who asked. He was generous, even when he shouldn't have been, and at one point he nearly lost his property because he didn't understand land taxes or banking. When he died, they found hundreds of uncashed checks among his things, which he had taken as payment for seedlings and produce.

In a book on the story of Deland and Lake Helen published in 1928, the daughter of Henry Addison Deland proudly held Lue Gim Gong up as part of Deland's citrus history, mentioning him and the orange he'd developed that, by this time, had spread throughout the state. But when the destitute Gong died in 1925, he had no headstone to mark his passing.

That changed when a few years after his death, a northerner came to pay his respects to the legendary figure of agriculture and was horrified to find no headstone. In the years since, the City of Deland has been happy

Mural of Lue Gim Gong, no longer standing, that used to be in Deland. *West Volusia Historical Society.*

to celebrate this eccentric genius of the grove and earth, so you'll now find a proper grave marker in Oakdale Cemetery, often included in tours from the West Volusia Historical Society, which has a display case of Lue's death mask, his 1911 Silver Pomological Medal and a memorial bust of Lue outside in a gazebo.

THE HAMLIN ORANGE

One of the oldest orange types in Florida still around is the Hamlin, which we can trace back to West Volusia County, near the town of Glenwood, on land sold to A.G. Hamlin by Henry Deland himself. A.G. Hamlin cultivated it in the late 1870s, and it became a rival of the Parson Brown after the Big Freeze. It's more widely found today than the Parson Brown.

Hamlin oranges, although you may buy them out of hand at fruit packing and U-pick farms, make for a better juicing orange than eating orange. They aren't as juicy as Valencias and are less tart, more mild in flavor, but they are a great choice for home-squeezed oranges, yielding a pale, sweet orange juice. If you like less acidic juice, these are the oranges for you. In Florida, they're firmly thought of as a bad prospect for eating, but in more arid climes, where the fruit is smaller, less juicy and the flavor more concentrated, they are decent for eating.

Because they are so juicy, they're denser and heavier than an eating orange. A midsize Hamlin's about two to three inches in diameter and seedless inside—well, nearly, as they're officially considered a seedless variety, but once in a while you'll encounter a seed.

EAST CENTRAL FLORIDA TODAY

Although rich in history, the geographic area of East Central Florida doesn't have nearly the number of counties or total acreage of Central Florida, but you can find Indian River oranges and citrus today in country stands and stores from Orlando to Miami and beyond. Although there are oranges that go to juice here, what the region is known for are its whole oranges—for quality, not quantity. St. Lucie County had a respectable 1,391,000 boxes of oranges in the citrus report from the 2016–17 year (about 2 percent of Florida's known commercial orange output). Indian River country had 1,176,000 boxes of oranges, Okeechobee had 502,000 boxes, Volusia had 67,000 boxes and Brevard had 94,000 boxes. To give some perspective, 68,750,000 boxes of oranges were recorded to have come out of Florida in 2016–17. Some thirteen counties hit above 1,000,000 boxes, with only three counties above 10,000,000 boxes.

For the orange tourist, there are plenty of wonderful stops in this region. One of the most notable is Al's Red Barn Grill—not only does it feature a fruit farm shop and handmade fudge, but it's also a restaurant serving Mexican food, breakfast fare and American food.

ON THE EDGE OF IT ALL
IN SOUTHEAST FLORIDA

The fickle fingers of frost doomed much of Florida orange production in the deep freeze of 1894–95, but far south, on the Miami River, an unaffected grove bloomed in view of a great swamp. A young widow carefully cut off the most beautiful and fruitful branch she could find, loaded down with blossoms and fruit. Then she sent it to the branch to Mr. Flagler at Palm Beach, with a note to say that if he brought his railroad down to the river, she would give him a square mile on the north bank. The area where the grove was is known now as Coconut Grove, a neighborhood of Miami, and the Widow Julia Tuttle wasn't the only one to entice Flagler with a gift of land—William Brickell also offered a large tract south of the river.

This story, a gift of a branch full of blossoms and fruit to lure the railway baron south, may be a fiction that's passed into legend, but the offer of land is certain. The fact that the frosts had not touched what would become Miami did make Flagler reconsider his original terminus at West Palm. He'd eventually push all the way to Key West, finishing his Over-the-Sea Extension in 1912.

Dade County didn't have very many white settlers in the late 1800s. The Indian Wars in the 1830s and '40s had pushed the Native Americans left down south and deep into the Everglades, and the isolated farmsteads on the edge of the swamp and sea soon found themselves under attack.

Late 1890s Palm Beach progressed mightily, especially after Flagler made it his terminus of the railway, before the Big Freeze changed his mind and he extended the line. Prior to Flagler's involvement, an early Palm Beach

FLORIDA ORANGES

settler was Robert McCormick, who built his home on the shores of Lake Worth. The mild microclimate between the Lake and the Atlantic Ocean made it perfect for McCormick's tropical garden, with everything from royal poinciana and coconut palms to citrus fruits. Flagler bought McCormick's land for his grand mansion, and as soon as that fact was publicized, land speculators began capitalizing on it—where Flagler bought land, development was sure to follow, as it did when he became interested in St. Augustine a decade before.

Some early orange groves prior to the mid-1800s were started in the Florida Keys on Indian Key by Dr. Henry Perrine, a noted botanist who managed an experimental station growing tropical plants and trees. But in 1840, nearly all the settlers and horticulturalists were killed by Native Americans, and it was abandoned as an experimental growing station. The wreck salvager and his wife who had lived there escaped, along with Perrine's family, but the botanist himself was reportedly hacked to pieces.

After the Great Freeze, though, things had changed, and even Henry Flagler had some groves down south, a seventy-acre lot between Homestead and Miami. The decade after the Big Freeze was a cold one, and another freeze in 1897 sealed Dade and Broward's reputation as practically frostproof.

Volusia County growers, like E.T. King and Philemon Bryan, made their way down after the Big Freeze to try their hands at farming oranges farther south in what would become Broward County. King brought his family down only once the railway had been completed to Fort Lauderdale, as the travel would have been too arduous before then.

DRAINING THE SWAMP, 1906–20

The Everglades on the Southeast portion of the state made for miry land, useless for settling and useless for growing anything in quantity except perhaps rice. The politician Napoleon Bonaparte Broward, for whom the county of Broward would be named, had a plan—a literal draining of the swamp. As this was an expensive enterprise, the tax base of Florida could not possibly absorb the cost. What was needed was more people and more money. Governor Broward's plan solved both. The state would sell the land under the murky waters ahead of the draining at a cheap price, using the sales to finance the draining. The ownership of the land would draw more people, increasing the tax base for the most Southeast counties and the state.

124

By 1906, Governor Broward had launched dredges to dig drainage canals. Optimistically, the planners of these canals believed that they would be used for easy egress throughout the city of Fort Lauderdale, which would be a veritable "Venice of America." Alas, this was not to be, as unforeseen issues of constant maintenance came up—not only water flowed into the canals but also silt, making the waterways too shallow for anything of size to pass through unless they were dredged constantly. As early as 1912, many canal transport routes silted to the point that steamboat travel was no longer possible. The last commercial passenger boat used the drainage canals in December 1921.

Although swamp draining proved more of an engineering feat than it had first appeared, Governor Broward's scheme seemed to have worked, and those who had bought huge swaths of land began reselling them, kicking off the start of the Florida Land Boom.

THE BOOM BEGINS, 1910–26

The Florida Land Boom was centered on Southeast Florida, although the ripples of it spread across the state, pushing real estate even in Central Florida. In the 1920s, it reached a fever pitch, but it began as early as 1908 and had picked up steam by 1910.

Evidence of that was the tent city of Progresso in 1911, as Broward's grand drainage plan was nearing completion. A good three to five thousand people could be found there camped in tents. The largest purchaser of the formerly undrained swamp was a land speculator named Richard Bolles, and he was the reason why thousands had flocked to Progresso. He sold lots twenty-five feet wide in Progresso for $240, a definite profit since he had picked them up at a mere $2 per acre from the state. But he added in a bit of marketing genius (which ended up being not quite legal): anyone who bought a lot had a chance to win up to 630 acres more in a lottery drawing.

Bolles told his prospective settlers in pamphlets and ads that the muck revealed by the draining could grow anything. He based his optimism on a report that had actually been blocked from publication for two full years by the Department of Agriculture for its overblown claims. But the Wright report was finally released, so Bolles and men like him, interested in selling or promoting the land, used it as the basis for their glowing advertisements. Although it was fertile, the muck wasn't the miracle they'd made it out to be, as it was later proven that it did not contain all the nutrients necessary to grow many vegetable crops. Many of the landowners also found that the land they'd bought from Bolles was underwater because the drainage wasn't yet complete, one of many reasons he ended up in court for fraud.

While Central Florida growers fretted over a freeze, it was rainstorms that made the Broward farmer anxious. In a 1982 interview (by Victoria Wagner), an old farmer, Ed Viele of Davie in Broward County, recalled the times, first as a child when he was brought in 1912 by his father, who had been drawn in with the promise of cheap land:

> *"As soon as our house was built, we started raising vegetables. No matter what your occupation or profession had been previously, here you raised tomatoes, cucumber, broccoli, and took them by boat to Ft. Lauderdale to be shipped north. But it was a pretty precarious business. Our land is only five feet above sea level here, and with heavy rains or strong winds we are inundated. At first, the horses and mules had to wear 'muck' shoes to keep from sinking knee deep in the heavy wet soil. Then the occasional frost finished the situation. We would have to begin all over again. It can be pretty depressing,"* he said, remembering those early days.

While family farmers toiled, land speculation gained speed. One real estate broker of Dade County interviewed in the 1940s said that during the 1920–26 boom, he had known a particular piece of land near Miami, starting at $250 per acre, to change hands several times, selling ultimately at $5,000 per acre and, once the boom went bust, to have passed back into the hands of the original owner, back at the value of $190 per acre, all within the span of two years.

Central Florida benefited from the land boom, and it had its own binder boys to meet the incoming speculators, selling the chance or binder to even buy land just as they did in Southeast Florida. But there was not enough development and industry for Dade, Broward and Palm Beach Counties to weather the loss in the same way as counties such as Polk had, although Boca Raton continued to be a playground for the rich and famous even after the heyday of the 1920s.

The cause of the land boom and the bust finally got traced back to unscrupulous bankers, sixty years after the bust, when a historian named Robert Vickers demanded the records be opened to the public. His book, *Panic in Paradise*, lays out the utter corruption, as banking insiders and politicians looted bank funds for their own gain. In Boca Raton, Addison Mizner funded his dream of developing the area with depositors' money once wealthy supporters began shying away. The regulators and government officials, meant to stem corruption, instead joined in on the reckless speculation and getting "loans" that were really payoffs from the very institutions they were supposed to be watching, then misleading the public for as long as possible about the state of things. When the supposedly stable Mizner Development Company was sued for fraud in 1926, it touched off a panic, with depositors throughout the Florida and Georgia banking systems demanding their funds. Comptroller Ernest Amos should have removed those bank officers who had given themselves illegal loans, damaging capital beyond what the laws of Florida allowed, but he, too, was part and parcel of a corrupt system. Even the governor of Florida at the time had been on the take.

By 1925, the wild land speculation, kept unnaturally afloat by dishonest money men, had begun to affect the railways. Thinking that the boom would last forever, brokers began ordering excess supplies—with trainloads of stock and building material shipped out with no particular destination on the manifest. Thousands of unclaimed freight boxes occupied every available inch of tracks in the train yards, taking up valuable cars needed for actual supplies. In October 1925, the Big Three (Flagler's Florida East Coast Railway, Plant's Atlantic Coast Line Railroad and Seaboard Air Line Railroad) suspended all outgoing freight except essentials for agriculture, fuel, food and livestock. Meanwhile, up in the northern states, bad press started churning regarding the shaky ground the boom was built on, warning investors off. With building supplies mostly blocked by the railway, developers still going forward with their projects now relied on the channel route connecting through Biscayne Bay. An old Danish warship, the massive *Prins Valdemar*, which was to be converted into a sort of floating hotel, capsized at the entrance in January 1926. It took six weeks for the ship to be righted and moved. As this was now the only route into Miami for large goods to come through, the *Prins Valdemar* not only sealed off Miami but also sealed the doom of the boom.

"The Big Blow," a massive hurricane in late 1926, furthered a lack of northern investors in Southeast Florida land. In September, the unnamed hurricane hit Fort Lauderdale, Dania and Hollywood and pummeled Miami worst of all. Most of the residents hailed from elsewhere and hadn't experienced the full force of a bad hurricane. A smaller hurricane had brushed by Broward County in July, damaging only Tent City, a canvas motel on Hollywood Beach. This lulled the residents into a false sense of security, so they were little prepared when the September hurricane hit.

Worse still, residents didn't yet understand the shape of the storm, and many of them came out into the open thinking the worst was over, only to be caught outdoors and drowned in their cars after the eye of the storm passed over. Casualties resulted—numbers reported at the time were between 327 and 650 dead, with more than 800 others not accounted for. Winds reached 150 miles per hour, leveling buildings, destroying windows and flooding the Broward Hotel four feet high in the lobby— enough that a building inspector ordered all the women and children be moved to the Women's Club on Andrews Street in Fort Lauderdale. By one account, the storm washed a family's Chrysler Imperial out of their garage and buried it in the sand deeply enough that it took two men three days to dig it out. Back in cities such as Philadelphia, exaggerated reports of casualties (in the thousands instead of the hundreds) added to the bad press the area was already getting from the bust of the land boom and all the bank failures.

Davie farmer Ed Viele recalled the damage he saw personally in 1926:

> *"Then, just as we were well started, and my groves were beginning to bear fruit—without such warning reports as we now have—a hurricane descended upon us.... The top of this house was blown off," he said, looking up with the memory of shock. "There were three feet of water in front of this house," he reached forward as if seeing it now. "We tried to save some of our plants by moving them up to the higher ground on the canal banks, but the cattle had taken refuge there as well as the wild cats, deer and snakes of the flooded Everglades. The plants were trampled; we lost everything and had to make a fresh start."*

It's easier to make a fresh start with vegetables, but oranges take years of cultivation and years after that before they have the best years of bearing. The hurricane and the end of speculation dealt the area a double blow. But out of the sodden mess of 1926, hope sprouted, mainly in the form of those who saw the low prices of the bust as an opportunity rather than an obstacle.

AFTER THE LAND BOOM BUSTED, 1926–40

When the land boom busted, one of the men who saw opportunity was Floyd L. Wray. He'd briefly been part of the crack sales team formed by Joseph W. Young, selling houses and land at Hollywood-by-the-Sea in the thick of the boom. When the job disappeared in 1926, Wray and his wife partnered with horticulturist Frank Stirling, buying 320 acres of land west of Davie, to be developed into orange groves.

Wray then pulled together a sales team of nine, partially drawn from the Hollywood-by-the-Sea salesforce. The Howey-in-the-Hills sales model most definitely inspired how they sold the land.

Instead of selling the land and walking away, they sold it as an investment property, or a "citrus condominium" program. Five-acre units were sold on five-year contracts for about $750 per acre, with Flamingo Groves responsible for planting and upkeep of the groves. At the end of the five years, the owners of the unit could either sell the units back to the owners at a pre-specified price (at a sure profit to the owners) or keep a prorated share of profits from the overall crop.

At first, all oranges planted on the profit-bearing part of the groves were late summer oranges, as Wray sought to capitalize on the open market. Wray was quoted as saying, "The shortage of oranges in Florida in the summer months and their extremely high prices during that season, caused me to establish a forty-acre grove of Lue Gim Gong summer maturing oranges on the black soils of the Everglades in the Davie area, where I found that a combination of mild temperature, moisture in abundance at all times and the organic soils, permitted the raising of an orange of superior flavor and juice content and at a minimum cost."

At the groves, Wray enlisted the help of Frank Stirling, a horticulture expert tasked with solving citrus blight by U.S. Department of Agriculture and Florida State Plant Board in the early 1900s. Among his many other accomplishments, Stirling would go on to be the first mayor of Davie. He helped set up and care for those first forty acres and a plot with at least sixty varieties of citrus grown on it for Flamingo Groves. By the 1930s, they had also had a botanical garden with exotics from around the world, given to them for testing by the USDA. It was spoken of as an experimental grove and garden in the press, which helped garner publicity for the sales promotions, as did the outdoor picnics and early tours.

Wray, Stirling and others still touted the miracle of the muck soils built from the decayed vegetable matter and silt of the Everglades, but there were issues when it came to orange growing. Citrus grew well to start, though later in the grove's life, soil had to be amended to make up for missing micro-elements, such as copper. Despite fantastic claims in the press, in a 1928 paper for the *Florida Horticultural Society Proceedings*, Stirling admitted that, though rich, muck land did need fertilizer. This is probably down to the press's tendency to quote only mostly exaggerated and positive statements to promote the area at the time.

The first worry, though, was the possibility of flood and storms, the humidity making the oranges vulnerable to fungi and bacteria. An orange grown in 'Glades muck tends to be less beautiful, without the fruit basket–worthy skins because of the damp, but the taste of a muck-grown orange is sweeter. This sweetness made it valuable to later orange juice concerns looking to balance out the high-acid fruits out of Polk County for a consistent blend of flavor for their brand.

Wray and Stirling's promotion of the land and, more importantly, the opening of the first modern packinghouse in Broward encouraged others to set out groves in the '30s. They advertised Florida citrus outside of Florida as well. In Chicago at the 1933–34 World's Fair, Florida had a pavilion on the Navy Pier, and all of the orange trees used to landscape the pavilion were shipped from Flamingo Groves, which also had its own exhibit within the pavilion.

Florida's 1933–34 World's Fair Exhibition. *Flamingo Gardens Archives, Davie, Florida.*

Above: Moving an orange tree
at Flamingo Groves. Many
were moved for exhibitions.
*Broward County Historical Archives,
Hollywood (FL) Souvenir Collection.*

Right: Image of Frank Lloyd Wray
as commissioner in 1931. *Flamingo
Gardens Archives, Davie, Florida.*

Not only did Wray manage his own groves and those of the investors, but because Flamingo Groves had all the equipment, infrastructure and employees already, he also ended up profiting somehow from nearly all the groves in the county, eventually thousands of acres—whether it be through management or services, through the packinghouse or shipping. The packinghouse was even conveniently right up against the railroad tracks, so it could load directly on to the cars.

In his position as an elected commissioner, Wray improved shipping overall for Southeast Florida, pushing for the small Lake Bay Mabel Harbor to become the massively expanded Port Everglades, getting the rail line extended so that fruit could be more easily moved to be shipped to sea.

In about 1939, Flamingo Groves grew to seven hundred acres, and by then, the experimentation on the orange groves had expanded to include reporting to other organizations such as the Belle Glade Experiment Station, the Florida State Experiment Station and the Florida State Fertilizer Institute.

FIGHTING THE RAIN, 1940s–1980s

Every orange grower in Florida past or present, east or west, dreads storms. A hurricane or tropical storm shakes the unripe fruit from the trees, damages orange skins and invites pathogens such as citrus canker, and too much rainfall can sink a crop. The modern farmer employs pumps to guard against it being too wet (for an orange tree needs good drainage), but even today, they would have probably been helpless against the rains of 1947.

In May 1947, it started raining, and it kept raining. Throughout the season, multiple storm systems soaked South Florida, hitting the average yearly rainfall with three months still left in the rainy season. The ground, already sodden from the previous deluges, could not absorb the eleven inches of rain the Category 4 hurricane left in just three hours. Compared to the 1926 Hurricane, loss of life was significantly lower, probably because the populace had learned from that storm and others (such as the 1928 Category 5 Hurricane that wiped out Belle Glade in Palm Beach County, killing thousands) and because storm warnings and communications significantly improved in the twenty years since. Residents fled from the floods, ending up in temporary camps until the waters drained, and the U.S. government literally called in the cavalry, sending in amphibious vehicles, men on horseback and army manpower. Fields lay underwater when planting was set to begin, cattle died and partially built roads washed away, although only seventeen Floridians reportedly died. The Davie area had already lost thirty-five thousand citrus trees due to the rains, and the storm ruined much of what was left.

Stan Wood, a relation of the Wrays, grew up in the groves (later getting into the citrus industry himself and taking on the role of executive director of Flamingo Gardens) and remembered the flooding in '47. He was no more than seven years old, tromping around in his father's rain boots, looking at all the thousands of drowned earthworms in wonder. The water didn't come up over the boots, but it flooded at least a foot deep even up on the higher ground of hammock ridge where most of the groves were. Being so young, he wasn't aware of what a blow it had been to orange growing until he investigated later: "I read all the corporate minutes from the '30s on and you can see that the spirit of the endeavor was deflated after that '47 flood. [Before that] every one of those annual reports were just nothing but optimism." Still, he said, in the 1950s and '60s, citrus was "a booming thing." The flooding led to the formation of the Central and South Florida Flood Control District, now the South Florida Water Management District.

The Panhandle and the western Florida coast also experienced citrus damage, with Pinellas County losing 75 percent of the year's crop, although damage to the trees themselves in this area was negligible. It was not the first time a storm had shaken the citrus farmers of Florida, and it was far from the last.

Storms weren't the only weather-related trial. Freezes occasionally reached down to the southern portion of the state, although it was never as damaging for citrus growers as it was in the more northern parts of Florida. If they could save the fruit and trees, through firing and other techniques, the loss from the other parts of the state pushed the price of oranges up. The year 1934 saw a reading of twenty-eight degrees at Miami International Airport, a temperature in the danger zone for freezing an orange solid (generally between twenty-six and twenty-eight degrees). Other record lows in the area included just thirty-one degrees in West Palm in 1940, twenty-seven degrees in 1977 and, of course, in the 1980s, that terrible decade, thirty-one in 1986 and twenty-eight on Christmas Day 1989. Christmas 1989 saw somewhat higher temperatures a little farther south: thirty-five degrees in Fort Lauderdale, thirty-four in Hollywood and thirty-eight at Miami Beach.

Wood, who turned from helping manage the orange trees at Flamingo Groves as a young man to opening his own citrus-based business, Everglades Botanical, in 1969, said that growers in Southeast Florida "spent a lot of time thinking about the freezes, because it was so profitable for us. One cold night and the value in your crop doubled," and down south it hardly ever froze long enough and hard enough for it to be a real danger to oranges.

Oranges and the orange groves were a component of Florida tourism by the '50s and '60s, something that Flamingo Groves (later to be renamed Flamingo Gardens) capitalized on. The collection of tropical and subtropical plants and trees established at the Groves brought tourists in, and they added a bird sanctuary. Each year, they sent out their orange catalogues to the Midwest and northern states—although they sold from their own groves, they also marketed and sold the sought-after Indian River fruit.

Palm Beach's citrus industry has always been dwarfed by its sugarcane and vegetable crop. In the late '50s and early 1960s, Palm Beach had about one-fourth of the orange acreage that Broward did in bearing trees. But by 1971, Palm Beach County had more citrus acreage than Broward and Dade put together. Palm Beach surpassed Broward in the late 1960s in orange production and continued to do so for decades. By the 1970s, Dade County had no commercial orange groves, its citrus being limes and lemons.

Flooding in the late 1970s led to more funding for efficient pumping systems and canals in Dade and Broward County. The worst of it came in 1979. Unlike in 1947, when he was a child without a care in his father's rain boots, Stan Wood was now a citrus grower. He calls the flood of 1979 "probably the most traumatic thing I've been through, other than the death

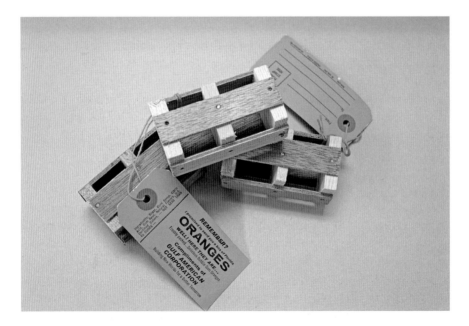

Above: Flamingo Groves–branded playing cards. *Broward County Historical Archives, Hollywood (FL) Souvenir Collection.*

Opposite: Orange-related novelty items like this tiny 1966 crate, originally filled with orange gumballs, were sold in Florida. *Broward County Historical Archives, Hollywood (FL) Souvenir Collection.*

of my mother." Although he still runs Everglades Botanical and is on the board of Flamingo Gardens, he got out of orange groves in 1988, saying, "I was in it about nine years longer than I should have been."

Profitable development claimed more and more of citrus lands in Broward in the 1980s, especially around Flamingo Gardens. To make way for an airport, the on-site packinghouse was closed and demolished in 1984.

THE AGE OF CANKER ERADICATION, 1995–2006

A bout of citrus canker broke out in Miami in 1995—not in commercial groves at first, but mainly in dooryard or residential trees. A bacterial infection, canker shows itself as lesions on the fruit and young stems and leaves, mostly brownish in color, with a yellowish edge. The worst cases can lead to defoliation, root rot and early fruit drop. Highly contagious, canker can be spread by wind-borne rain, people carrying the infection on their person or equipment or by moving infected or exposed plants or plant parts. In early stages, the fruit is edible—just not all that pretty—but the spread of canker can weaken trees and make them susceptible to other things. For the fruit basket industry, it's particularly bad, but it's something a juice grove can live with.

From September 1995 to December 1999, any tree within 125 feet of an infected tree was destroyed. In 2000, the state took the extreme measure of destroying any tree within 1,900 feet of an infected tree, even if it was perfectly healthy. To give you some idea of the scale, a football field is 300 feet long, and 1,900 feet is more than six times that.

It's arguable as to whether the policy of total eradication was the best plan to contain the epidemic, although there were successes—citrus growers pointed to Hillsborough County, which submitted to the 1,900 rule, as being canker free by 2001 as a result of the program. At the very least, it's a hotly contested point. In his many papers and articles on the problem in the 1980s, canker expert plant pathologist Jack Whiteside put forth the theory that an eradication program would be more disruptive and costly than simple management with sprays and that conditions in Florida aren't as conducive to canker most seasons as it is in places such as Argentina. Canker can kill a tree, it's true, but mostly if it already has other problems or has gone almost completely untreated. Official state experts, however, were ready to destroy even seemingly healthy trees, contending that their actions were necessary to save the industry and that living with canker would cost the industry more than eradication.

Lesions on the leaves and fruit leave a tree more vulnerable to canker, and it was just Florida's luck that citrus leaf miners had invaded the state as well. Wet conditions, enough wind to batter the fruit and leaf miners to introduce the bacteria to tender young leaves had, in the minds of state officials, created a perfect storm. Worse still, they knew that bad weather, like a hurricane, could spread the pathogen much farther than the 1,900 feet they'd determined. This wasn't an arbitrary number, but one borne out of scientific study, as well as the long lead time between infection and symptoms.

The state began its citrus eradication program in 2000, going into the yards of private homes without permission, in counties such as Palm Beach, Broward, Lee and Dade. Dooryard citrus trees were destroyed, but not without protests from the homeowners. Fifty-eight thousand Broward households were affected by the eradication program.

Property laws and compensation for the confiscation or destruction of private property were at issue here, and the courts mostly found in favor of the homeowners. In Broward for instance, in May 2002, a judge ruled inspectors could not enter the yard of a private homeowner without a signed waiver. Courts also ruled that homeowners were due compensation for the trees. That didn't mean they got paid, however. Because the state did not approve the payouts, homeowners had to wait years. Broward County residents, for instance, won a jury verdict from the Florida Department of Agriculture and were eventually put in the state budget, but Governor Rick Scott vetoed the payment nearly ten years after the verdict. The Supreme Court of Florida upheld his ability to do so in a 6–1 decision.

The state finally gave up the eradication program in 2005–6 after hurricanes came through and spread canker so much throughout the state that they decided on management instead. They blamed homeowners blocking the destruction of trees for the spread, saying that those trees were the reason canker was still present to be spread, while others still argued that eradication was nearly impossible and that the high winds and moisture made for a perfect breeding ground.

CITRUS TODAY IN SOUTHEAST FLORIDA

Dade and Broward haven't been included in the USDA Florida Citrus reports of the last few years because so little is being produced. The decline and disappearance of orange groves is likely due to a combination of flooding issues, storms, the destruction of most trees during the 1990–2000s outbreaks of canker and rising real estate prices competing with farmland. Most who did keep their dooryard trees gave up with the break out of citrus greening.

Only twelve thousand boxes came out of Palm Beach County in the 2008–9 season, and in the past few years (2015–18), if the USDA's citrus report for Florida does include Palm Beach, it's generally lumped in with another county because of the low numbers these days. Most of what is grown today as far as fruit in Palm Beach are exotics and tropicals—star fruit, guava, dragon fruit, kumquats, mangos, avocados and the like.

Flamingo Gardens, which changed its name from Flamingo Groves in the late 1970s, no longer grows oranges today. As the industry diminished in the county due to age, canker and greening, many of its orange trees were replaced by mango, and Hurricane Wilma in 2005 did the rest in. Until Wilma, it still sold fruit and fresh juice and did gift fruit shipping during the holidays.

Even though you won't find oranges on site today, it's worth going to tour the Wray Home Museum and checking out the narrated tram tour at Flamingo Gardens. The Wray Home Museum exhibitions include Wray family portraits, panoramic photos of the groves, thank-you letters from President and Mrs. Eisenhower for delivery of fruit and memorabilia from the retail outlets in Broward County. The narrated tram tours also give a historic perspective of the groves and gardens.

Other attractions at the gardens include botanical gardens with rare, exotic and native plants, a wildlife sanctuary that gives residence to permanently injured native wildlife, a free-flight aviary with one of the largest collections of wading birds in America and informative wildlife encounter shows.

Two spots along Griffin Road in Broward county are a must-stop if you're a culinary tourist interested in citrus. The first is Spyke's Grove, which has been around for seventy years. While they don't grow oranges on site, they do grow other citrus and will carry nursery plants, and during the orange season, they pack out a lot of gift baskets from Indian River, some of which is grown by family members, and you can order from them or buy onsite. There's also a Koi farm next door.

The second is Bob Roth's New River Groves, more of the traditional, old-school citrus shop for tourists and those who want fresh, Florida-grown oranges. But it also has some delightful homemade pies that locals like to buy, especially during the holiday season, and it has stone crabs during season.

It's much easier to buy one of Terry's Famous Homemade Pies at Bob Roth's New River Groves Shop, but I've included a recipe with my own take on an Orange Key Lime Pie, in case you're far away from South Florida!

Orange Key Lime Pie

1 graham cracker crust (store-bought, or you can make your own)
1 can (14 ounces) sweetened condensed milk
4 egg yolks
¼ cup and 1 tablespoon freshly squeezed orange juice (about 2–3 oranges)
¼ cup and 1 tablespoon freshly squeezed lime juice (about 3 limes)
1 ¼ cups chilled heavy cream
6 tablespoons powdered sugar
optional: 1–2 tablespoons grated orange zest

Preheat oven to 350 F. If you are conserving oranges, before you squeeze (if you are going to use the zest as a topping later), zest what you want before squeezing the oranges. Make sure only to take the colored portion and not the bitter white pith. Store the zest in the fridge in a ziplock bag with the air pushed out of it, until needed.

You don't really have to worry about the exact ratio of lime to orange juice (except to your own personal taste) as long as the total volume of juice equals ½ cup and 2 tablespoons. For a sweet, all-orange pie, you'd need about 3–4 large oranges. If you're feeling creative, you can even fill in with a little lemon juice—again, as long as the total amount of juice is ½ cup and 2 tablespoons. Squeeze what you need and set aside.

Mix the condensed milk and yolks with a whisk until combined evenly. Add all your juices now. Pour filling into pie crust and bake in the middle of the oven for 15 minutes. Let set out of oven until it cools, then place in refrigerator overnight or a minimum of eight hours.

Beat cream and powdered sugar with an electric mixer, until it just holds slightly stiff peaks. Spread on top of pie. Top with grated orange zest if you would like.

CHALLENGES

For the past one hundred years, whenever the Florida citrus industry has faced a crisis, there's been one institution that's been the first line of defense: the Citrus Experiment Station, today known as the Citrus Research and Education Center, located in Polk County at Lake Alfred.

By 1917, citrus was the leading agricultural cultural crop in the state, but agricultural science and communication with growers lagged behind the need for research. The University of Florida already had its own research facility, but it didn't have a way to connect with growers on a large scale. In 1912, an outbreak of citrus canker began and then dragged on for several years, and a freeze in 1917 showed a clear need for a more official research facility to support citrus. Funding for the initial plots came from major growers in the state, with backing from state legislature.

The CREC's calendar of recommended fertilizer and pest control improved yields enough to build smaller farmers' trust through the 1920s and '30s. Over the years, it has fought all the various diseases, blights and citrus problems that cropped up over the decades and supported citrus farmers with scientific studies on best practices.

Visit the CREC today and you'll find a sprawling complex of buildings and experimental groves, with agricultural scientists dedicated to various specialties, from entomology to plant pathology. It's the largest single commodity research center in the world, with the largest library dedicated to citrus.

SOLVING GREENING

While the CREC studies all the pests and diseases that can plague citrus, its focus has shifted to one all-consuming purpose: solving the problem of citrus greening. The bacteria, spread by tiny psyllid bugs, attacks the inner bark and clogs the trees' "arteries," even to the roots, blocking the egress of water, needed nutrients and minerals. This causes a nutrient deficiency and eventually, in untreated cases, death from the inability to transport water to the branches and treetops properly.

An orange with a little green or yellow on it doesn't mean that the orange has greening—there's lots of reasons for a perfectly tasty and delicious orange to get a tinge of green on its skin, including a small temperature change. True untreated greening produces a fruit not just slightly yellow-green but stunted, asymmetrical and so bitter as to not be salable.

It's been more than a decade since the first hint of citrus greening showed up in Florida. Citrus greening is known by different names—HLB, or *huanglongbing*, which translates from the Chinese to "Yellow Dragon disease." First discovered by scientists in China during the late 1930s and '40s, because of Communism the information wasn't passed on to other countries for many years. In the 2004–5 growing season, scientists confirmed what Florida growers on the ground already suspected: greening had taken hold, and it was here to stay.

Greening steadily chipped away at Florida groves over the years. In a 2017 *Orlando Sentinel* article, Dr. Jacqueline K. Burns, dean for research with the University of Florida Institute of Food and Agricultural Sciences and director of the Florida Agricultural Experiment Station, said, "Altogether, citrus greening has reduced revenues from Florida processed orange and grapefruit production by $4.64 billion over the 10 seasons that the disease has affected production. Citrus greening has also cost the state $1.76 billion in labor income and more than 3,400 jobs."

When greening appeared, growers had just dealt with the canker epidemic, and that eradication effort killed thousands of Florida trees. Frightened owners began selling off groves, although many of the larger and generational growers still hung on. By February 2009, greening had spread to all commercial growing counties in the state of Florida. Many growers picked up other crops, while still maintaining orange groves, hoping that sales of various vegetables, blueberries and even olives might buoy them through the difficult times. Abandoned groves, not tended because the owners intended to sell, harbored bacteria-carrying psyllids, further spreading the disease.

One grower, Maury Boyd, rather than destroying the trees, which had been recommended to stop the spread, started treating his trees in the mid- to late 2000s. Many were angry at him for trying to treat rather than destroy, earning him the nickname "Typhoid Maury."

By the time greening showed up in his groves, Boyd believed that most of the state was infected, even if trees hadn't yet shown symptoms, and that it was too late for eradication, too late for quarantine. "The tipping point had arrived before we were even diagnosed," Boyd said in a 2013 *Huffington Post* article.

What was left was managing the symptoms. So that's what Boyd did, despite official protest. He began placing more nutrients and minerals, using vasodilators to open the bacteria-blocked tree arteries, treating aggressively with immune boosters and controlling the psyllid population with psyllid-targeted insecticide rather than older methods that killed even beneficial or innocuous bugs.

In 2012, his trees were doing better than they were before they were diagnosed with greening, with higher-quality fruit and better yields. His methods do nothing to curb the actual infection, so his trees are a vector of disease—a point of contention. And it's expensive. By 2013, the cost of maintaining groves was $1,900 per acre, twice what it was before greening, too much for many cash-strapped growers with groves already too far gone. Even with treatment, trees still can and do die from greening.

Growers throughout Florida have been using the Boyd Method or something like it, and despite all the massive drops in production, it's helped keep Florida in the citrus game, along with advances from UF's Citrus Experimental Station and Education Center.

For the 2016–17 season, California grew 51 percent of total United States citrus; Florida accounted for 45 percent, while Texas and Arizona produced the last 4 percent. Every year since greening came into effect, Florida's overall production has dropped, with each crop smaller than the year before. The 2017–18 season was the lowest production Florida's seen since the late 1940s, mainly because of greening, but largely because Hurricane Irma hit high-producing groves in the Southwest. For the first time since the late 1940s, California surpassed Florida's citrus production in the 2017–18 season.

THE FUTURE IN THE AGE OF GREENING

In 2018, when asked what percentage of trees are currently infected in the state of Florida, CREC's Director Dr. Michael Rogers answered, "Probably close to 100%, unless you've just put them in the ground."

Dr. Megan Dewdney, plant pathologist at the CREC, said that greening is a difficult bacteria to defeat and treat. It can't be grown in a petri dish, so pathologists have to study the effects in the trees themselves, and it's difficult to get samples from every part without damaging a tree. So she, and other scientists, have to mostly study the disease in the field. Even low levels of the bacteria can cause disruption in the tree, but it's also hard to study because the bacteria DNA still remains, even if they have killed it. Sometimes, she said, "It's like chasing shadows," and most of what they are doing currently is about masking the symptoms in a multi-pronged approach.

In the age of greening, said Dewdney, it's all about "keeping the plant stress-free in every respect." So growers have to look at every aspect of keeping the trees healthy, often using things long known but that were not important in other decades. There's been a resurgence in sour orange rootstocks over the past five years, especially around Indian River, because they grow very well in that area and may be greening-tolerant. Sour oranges were abandoned in past years because they lacked resistances to earlier scourges and diseases that, while still a threat, are better understood than greening and less of an immediate problem, so growers are willing to take the chance.

Unless smaller growers band together for more contiguous acreage, Dewdney said that most small growers would struggle. "If you're a small grower who has only 10–20 acres, you're almost dead in the water. The larger acreage you are, the better you're able to keep that core safe," said Dewdney, because greening tends to attack the borders of acreage, and massive growers (as in Brazil) have an easier time keeping the percentage of infection down, some as low as 1–2 percent.

One promising treatment from Southern Gardens Citrus (based out of Hendry County in Southwest Florida) involves a sort of inoculation. Testing is still in the beginning stages, so there isn't much information out there yet on the efficacy of treatment. It has applied to the U.S. Department of Agriculture for a permit of field trials in cooperation with CREC. Basically, Southern Gardens infects the tree with a weakened and modified version of another citrus scourge, called citrus tristeza virus, or CTV. The weakened strain delivers a spinach protein paired with it, and when that protein comes in contact with the bacterium that causes greening, the protein punches a hole in it, killing the bacterial cell. If it's successful, it might be a complete cure, although it will take a lot of time to fully test. It's not the only CTV-driven study or work that's going on, as the virus can be used to turn off or on gene sequences of interest, as well as introduce foreign sequences.

Killing the bacteria outright, managing psyllids, making sure trees have the right nutrition in smaller doses and growing the best trees for the land are all among the approaches being studied. But one lab at CREC isn't looking to kill greening—it wants to build a better tree. It is looking for both a rootstock and scion that are either highly tolerant or resistant to greening.

Drs. Fred Gmitter and Jude Grosser of CREC, known colloquially as the "Orange Brothers" (for their passion for oranges and their close relationship) are working to breed these oranges. Some of what they do is highly technical, such as giving an orange four parents instead of two. But they also do standard cross-breeding, trying to track the characteristics that might make a particular seedling tolerant to citrus greening. The disease involves so many mechanisms within the tree that it's difficult to pin their hopes on any one gene sequence, but if they do unlock something that makes a tree totally resistant or highly tolerant, they'll have to find more than one way to do it. As Dr. Grosser said, "You always need a backup method of resistance." That's because if the bacteria adapts to one in a few years, having another in place lengthens the amount of time it works. "Growers want a guarantee, so if we do manage it, that's how we'd have to do it," said Grosser.

More than a dozen rootstocks have been developed by the CREC and the Orange Brothers. They normally don't release them as early, but Dr. Gmitter said, "Desperate times call for desperate measures." Early testing indicates that these rootstocks might be tolerant, but they tell the farmers that CREC hasn't collected enough information to say that they are completely tolerant or even how they might behave in field testing. Farmers will plant early-release rootstocks and give them much-needed data.

They've also bred tolerant scions grafted onto the rootstock, the buds from which the oranges actually come. The one the Orange Brothers believe might be the best of them is the Sugar Belle Mandarin variety, a tangy-sweet eating orange, a mix of the sweet Clementine and the colorful, bell-shaped Minneola. Scientists are still studying why these scions are moderately tolerant. Tolerance doesn't mean that the oranges, both the scions and the rootstock, don't get greening—it just means that they handle it better.

What the scientists at CREC do agree on is that while greening might not be cured for years, Florida has turned the corner on learning to manage it. Without Hurricane Irma in the 2017–18 season, they felt that the numbers on production would have held steady for the first time in years rather than dropping, and barring other disasters, they are hopeful that the 2018–19 season should be a good one.

SOUTHWEST FLORIDA

The New Center of Oranges

For the past sixty years, the center of orange growing has shifted. Although Central Florida still has the productively powerful Polk County, as well as many moderate producing counties, it is now the Southwest counties that often hold the top spots in orange production.

Earlier in history, Lee and Collier Counties got a bump in citrus production with the 1894–95 freezes, with predictions that the Caloosahatchee area would be the center of Florida citrus production. More than one hundred years later, this never came to pass, but Lee County orange numbers are respectable for the state at more than 1 million boxes. Collier is one of the larger players at an average of more than 5 million boxes in the state.

For most of the history of the Southwest counties of Lee, Collier, Hendry, Glades, Charlotte, DeSoto and Manatee, there wasn't very much of a volume in orange production compared to the rest of the state.

Freezes higher in the state through the first half of 1900s had growers, especially those with larger concerns, eyeing the land in these more southern countries. Land in Hendry County was especially hard to come by, and in the early 1950s, most of the acreage was owned by only a few families (perhaps as few as seven families). There was land in Southwest Florida, but it just didn't change hands often and was mostly used for cattle.

A grower named Bob Paul during the 1950s already had a small patch (a grapefruit grove between Fort Myers and La Belle Florida) that he'd started up in 1938, and he'd also seen old-growth trees untouched by frost. He teamed up with another farmer to buy 160 acres in 1956, and in about 1960, he bought land south of La Belle.

But in 1962, he'd probably felt he'd finally hit the jackpot when he'd heard of 16,965 acres for sale in Hendry. It was part of a parcel of 80,000 acres owned by the Nocatee-Manatee Crate Company, which had used the land to grow pine wood for fruit crates. As it was such a large purchase, he ended up putting in with other citrus growers Jack Berry Sr. and Winston Lawless, along with securing financing. Bob Paul had the first section planted by 1964, and in less than a decade, Hendry County would go from minor player to major player in the citrus industry.

Although growers were slowly moving down in the 1950s, it was the freeze of 1962 that caused the biggest push to the Southwest counties. Berry (one of the three growers who had bought land with Paul) decided on expanding to Hendry after his groves at Lake Alfred froze to a chilling twelve degrees Fahrenheit. In *A History of Florida Freezes*, Bob Paul's son, Gene, related that when his father decided to get more land in the 1960s, Bob said this: "Gene, there aren't any big tracts of good citrus land left in Polk County. We've got to go either north, or south. To the north, there's good land around Ocala and Brooksville—but it's cold. Down south it's wet, but I can feel water and move it. I can't move cold. We're going south."

Some of the attractions at Mixon Fruit Farms. *Mixon Fruit Farms.*

147

Two of the counties here, DeSoto and Hendry, in recent growing seasons (2015–16 and 2016–17), produced the most boxes of oranges in the state.

While the majority of the growers in the Southwest run large commercial concerns, there's still history, particularly in Arcadia. The Shelfer family has been growing oranges near Joshua Creek since the 1880s. Today, they run Joshua Citrus, a farm store that offers grove tours. They've started up a small Orange Blossom Festival that the local community enjoys as well.

The Citrus Place in Manatee County's Terra Ceia is said to be one of the best stops in the state for juice. It's a blend of whatever citrus tastes good and is available from grower Ben Tillet, whose family might go back in citrus as far as the 1880s. He produces fresh, unpasteurized juice by squeezing citrus at the shop, just south of the Sunshine Skyway Bridge in Manatee County.

Another must-stop in the area is Mixon Fruit Farms, in operation since 1939. It's got a tram grove tour, a place for kids to play, a wildlife refuge (with gators on site), orange juice wines, fresh OJ, fruit and jams. The location also rents out part of the grounds for events, in particular weddings.

THE VALENCIA ORANGE

One of the major motivators for the southerly move are Valencia oranges. As the orange juice market picked up speed in the 1950s, the Valencia emerged as the orange best suited to provide juice. But Valencias are late-season oranges, and most of the oranges on the tree won't be mature enough to pick until March. What that means for growers is that Valencias have to get through all of the freeze season, so it's in more danger—vulnerable longer than say, a Navel orange, which has a season of about November through January.

For growers in South Florida, east or west, especially around the 1930s, Valencias and late oranges such as the Lue Gim Gong (which was a Valencia hybrid) were the best choices. In that area of the state, there's less of a chance of a freeze getting cold enough to hurt the crop, but because early and mid-season oranges were so prevalent at the time, late-season oranges could demand higher prices.

As freezes became more frequent and Valencias became more and more popular throughout the state, it makes sense that growers would move south. Sweet and incredibly juicy, the Valencia is the most common orange in the state today.

SNAPSHOT: FOURTH-GENERATION GROWER PAUL MEADOR
OF EVERGLADES HARVESTING, 2018

Paul Meador peels citrus with the efficiency of a man who has done it a million times, a captivating spiral of orange sprouting from his pocket knife. There's a mundane magic to it, but for him it's ordinary.

Juice from the Valencia drips to the ground as he offers me a sweet slice from the top, cut across the segments. We're standing in one of his groves at the end of a row, by a lovingly protected twig of a shiny-leafed tree that's only one year old, right next to a tree that's twenty-seven years old.

It's a large grove, so big that he's got tanks of fuel on site for his workers' vehicles. He's planted mostly oranges, but off to the side he's diversified a little, growing bell peppers. Over the centuries, a lot of citrus growers have done the same, growing other crops that have a shorter growing time and less investment (like the celery farmers of Sanford) or getting into another agricultural field such as cattle. This helps growers like him put by a steady income for the disastrous years. Hurricane Irma hitting in 2017 made it one of those years.

Government help didn't come soon enough for a lot of growers. It was the first year since citrus greening that the crop had really turned around. In October, the Florida Department of Agriculture announced that Florida citrus damages from Irma were more than $760 million. "Those of us that carry insurance were going to get a fraction of what the crop was really worth....The disaster relief fund was finally appropriated in February, and the hurricane was in September," says Meador. Without relief, growers might sell the land to other industries with a smaller economic impact per acre such as cattle farming, and while growers wait for the money to be distributed, they get deeper in debt and are unable to pay for goods and services to sustain their groves. As of the first quarter of 2019, the federal relief had come through for most, but many growers were still waiting on the other half, funded by the State of Florida.

Near La Belle, where Meador has one of his groves, there's a large amount of commercial oranges these days. Meador explains that the Southwest doesn't have as much of history as far as oranges are concerned because it just wasn't possible before. He's been here since a freeze in the late '70s drove him down to look for warmer prospects. The ground, he said, tends to get too soppy in the wet season. To grow here, you've got to use heavy equipment to prepare the land for proper drainage with overall gradient, and that just was too difficult in the early days of citrus.

The rows of oranges and tangerines are planted on raised, tiny hills, with a path in the middle. The idea is that water will roll off the hills into the paths, and if that gets too wet, he's got pumps and canals to dump the water in, which have become a hangout for local birds.

Meador believes in being a responsible steward of the land. Environmentalist groups have complained about the impact of runoff fertilizer from the groves, but Meador says that he and other growers are very precise about what they place, giving the trees exactly what they'll need and absorb readily. Adding fertilizer just before a hard rain or too much for the trees to take in would just be a waste. "No grower wants to spend more than they have to on fertilizer," says Meador.

A lot of the original grove trees in Florida were fifty feet by fifty feet. In the old days, Meador remembers harvesting ladders from his childhood that were forty feet high. Over time, growers figured out that bigger wasn't always better, so Meador's trees and most modern groves are closer to twenty-two feet high and about ten feet wide. Trees are bred to be smaller, and growers use hedge toppers to keep height lower, with some groves having rounded tree tops and others flat, so that many groves start to look like giant hedges—all according to the grower's preference. "Everything's very sculpted now," says Meador.

Meador no longer fires his groves, exclusively using micro-irrigation to protect his trees. As he'd moved south, freeze dangers weren't so prevalent. Fuel for firing a grove is expensive, and micro-irrigation is more cost-effective and efficient. The micro-irrigation system is also a way to deliver precise nutrients and fertilizer to the trees. Although you'll find a few vintage smudge pots in old Central Florida groves, firing these days is extremely rare in Florida.

As we drive through the grove, I ask about those doomsayers who think that oranges in Florida are near to finished because of all the recent hardships. Paul smiles and says, "Well, you can see how I feel about that. I've planted young trees out here." One section of the grove features rows of two-year-old trees, and here and there are year-old trees. The way he sees it, in any endeavor there are optimists and pessimists. "The difference," he says, "is that the optimists are still in business."

ORANGE TOURIST STOPS

Citrus is seasonal, and some shops close postseason, so whatever the web might say about hours of operation, we suggest that you call ahead to check. The season is generally from October to November through the end of March, sometimes longer (through May or June) if they have Valencias, but changes season to season. We've gathered some of the shops, groves and orange destinations of interest, along with a few tourist spots of historical significance that might not have oranges on site. Always call ahead to confirm location and status.

CENTRAL AND NORTH CENTRAL FLORIDA

Citrus Tower of Clermont
141 North Highway 27, Clermont, FL 34711; (352) 394-4061
https://citrustower.com
No fresh citrus, but just a slice of old Florida orange culture, memorabilia, photos of what the view used to look like and tourist gift shop.

Cross Creek Groves
6609 U.S. 301, Hawthorne, FL 32640; (800) 544-8767
www.crosscreekgroves.com
Near Marjorie Kinnan Rawlings's groves from the 1930s—a great piece of old Florida!

Davidson of Dundee

28421 Highway 27 North, Dundee, 33838; (863) 439-1698
www.davidsonofdundee.com

The handmade citrus candies are a way to experience citrus culture in the off season and take it home without worrying about spoilage, but in season, Davidson has fresh fruit.

Florida's Natural Grove Store

20160 Highway 27 in Lake Wales, FL 33853; (863) 679-4110
floridasnaturalgrovehouse.com

Variety of products, from orange-based cleaners and orange-themed clothing to valuable vintage orange crate labels, edibles, gift baskets of oranges and more. Open October–May.

Florida Orange World

5395 West Irlo Bronson Memorial Highway, Kissimmee, FL 34746; 1-800-531-3182
www.orangeworld192.com

Opened in 1971, Orange World's claim to fame is being shaped like a giant orange. Great stop for fresh citrus and jams to take home!

Hollieanna Groves Shop & Packing House

540 South Orlando Avenue, Maitland, FL 32751; (407) 644-8803
www.hollieanna.com

In operation since 1954, it grows, picks and packs its own citrus. It guarantees its products!

Jennings Citrus

1230 South Main Street, Wildwood, FL 34785; (352) 748-5554
www.jenningscitrus.com

Open since 1949! Among the varieties it sells are Valencias, so it tends to be open a little later in the season than many other shops.

The Orange Shop

18545 U.S. 301, Citra, FL 32113; (352) 595-3361
www.floridaorangeshop.com

Established in 1936, it's a must-stop for the orange tourist!

Osceola County Historical Society Pioneer Village

2491 Babb Road, Kissimmee, FL 34746; (407) 396-8644
http://osceolahistory.org

No fresh oranges available, but there's an old citrus packing facility, along with a pioneer village.

Red Hill Groves Farm Store

7218 Ronald Reagan Boulevard, Sanford, FL 32773; (407) 885-0272
https://www.redhillgroves.com

Fresh Florida oranges in the season, juice, ice cream, barbecue, fresh eggs and onions.

Reed's Groves aka Hilltop Grove

16661 Southeast Highway 42, Weirsdale, FL 32195; (352) 427-7794
www.facebook.com/hilltopgroves

A U-Pick experience in Marion County, locally loved and periodically discovered by the tourist willing to search for it.

Ridge Island Groves

Haines City location—6000 Polk City Road, Haines City, FL 33844; (863) 422-0333
Clermont location—320 Highway 27 South, Clermont, FL 34714; (352) 242-1511
www.ridgeislandgroves.com

The Clermont location features an ice cream shop, and you absolutely need to try the Orange Dream soft serve. Any of the ice creams with fruit will include fresh fruit from the farm.

Showcase of Citrus

5010 U.S. Highway 27, Clermont, FL 34711; (352) 267-2597
www.showcaseofcitrus.com

It's got U-Pick citrus and Monster Trucks, tours of the 2,500-acre ranch, gem mining and room for a picnic. Fifteen minutes west of Disney World.

Sunsational Citrus

700 North Central Avenue, Umatilla, FL 32784; (352) 771-2013
www.sunsationalcitrus.com

Orange-flavored soft serve and oranges, and it has restored an old icon of orange history, the Big Orange!

SOUTHEAST FLORIDA

Bob Roth's New River Groves
5660 Griffin Road, Davie, 33314; (954) 581-8630
www.newrivergroves.com
On the same strip of road as Spyke's Grove, Bob's is a traditional, old-school citrus shop. Locally known for homemade pies, and it has stone crabs!

Flamingo Gardens
3750 South Flamingo Road, Davie, FL 33330; (954) 473-2955
www.flamingogardens.org/wray-home-museum.html
No oranges here anymore, but the Wray House is worth visiting for the historical artifacts on display in regards to citrus in Broward County and the Wray family, who were the driving force behind citrus in the county for decades.

Robert Is Here Fruit Stand
19200 Southwest 344 Street, Homestead, 33034; (305) 246-1592
www.robertishere.com
Features exotics such as star fruit, guava, dragon fruit, kumquats, mangos, avocados and the like, with a few Florida orange products—orange blossom honey, orange marmalades and sauces. Animal farm on site and fruit milkshakes. Oranges aren't the focus, but it's a fun stop.

Spyke's Grove
7250 Griffin Road, Davie, 33314; (954) 583-0426
www.spykesgrove.com
Open for seventy years! It doesn't grow oranges on site, but it does grow other citrus and carry nursery plants. During the season, it packs gift baskets from Indian River, some of which is grown by family members. Order or buy on site. Koi farm next door.

CENTRAL EAST FLORIDA

Al's Family Farms
2001 North Kings Highway, Fort Pierce, 34951; (772) 460-0556
www.alsredbarngrill.com
Farm store with handmade fudge and a variety of citrus; also a restaurant that sells Mexican food, breakfast and burgers.

Barbours Produce

2440 Northeast Indian River Drive, Jensen Beach, FL 34957; (772) 225-2156
Cash only, with a wide variety of well-priced produce. Parking sometimes a challenge.

Countryside Citrus

6325 Eighty-First Street, Vero Beach, FL 32967 (Westside); (772) 581-0999
3300 Ocean Drive Vero Beach, FL 32966 (Beachside); (772) 234-8299
www.countrysidecitrus.com
Westside open seasonally, while Beachside locale is open throughout the year. Hay rides at Westside and a turtle pond. Soft-serve cream and fresh citrus at both locations. Known at the beach for fresh-squeezed OJ and key lime pies.

Indian River Citrus Museum

2140 Fourteenth Avenue, Vero Beach, FL 32960; (772) 770-2263
www.veroheritage.org/CitrusMuseum.html
Small exhibit on the citrus industry, including citrus crate labels.

Nelson Family Farms

875 West Midway Road, Fort Pierce, FL 34982; (772) 464-2100
www.nelsonfamilyfarms.com
Open-air produce market—fruits, vegetables, house-roast coffee, citrus plants and pottery.

Pell's Citrus and Nursery

400 Doyle Road, Osteen, 32764; (407) 322-3873
www.pellcitrus.com
Citrus emporium on twenty-four acres selling trees, fresh-squeezed juices, oranges and grapefruits.

Poinsettia Groves

1481 U.S. Highway 1, Vero Beach, 32960; (800) 327-8624
www.poinsettiagroves.com
Ships fruit all over the country; loved by locals picking up fresh oranges in the season.

TerMarsch Groves

13900 U.S. Highway 1, Juno Beach, FL; (561) 626-1177

www.shipfloridaoranges.com

Candy shop, fresh fruit and an "Old Florida" family-run store, selling fruit and just-squeezed OJ.

West Volusia Historical Society

137 West Michigan Avenue; (386) 734-4765

www.delandhouse.com

Display of Lue Gim Gong's death mask, pictures, reference books and memorial bust outside.

WEST COAST

Boyett's Grove

4355 Spring Lake, Brooksville, 34601; (352) 796-2289

www.boyettsgrove.com

Gift shop featuring fruit, a dinosaur cave, mini golf, an aviary and a zoo where visitors can feed the animals.

Dooley Groves

1651 Stephens Road, Ruskin, FL 33570; (813) 645-3256

dooleygroves.com

Includes onsite U-Pick grove and farm store!

Florida Orange Groves Winery

1500 Pasadena Avenue South, St. Petersburg, 33707; (727) 347-4025

floridawine.com

Wines made from 100 percent Florida orange juice and other Florida fruit-based selections.

SOUTHWEST

The Citrus Place

7200 U.S. 19, Terra Ceia, FL 34250; (941) 722-6745

www.facebook.com/TheCitrusPlace

Known for its fresh citrus juice, a blend of whatever citrus is good and in season.

Joshua Citrus
4135 Southeast County Road 760, Arcadia, 34266; (800) 749-8219
www.joshuacitrus.com
Citrus, fresh juice, jams and ice cream. Holds grove tours and an annual Orange Blossom Festival. Family orange history goes back to the 1880s.

Mixon Fruit Farms
2525 Twenty-Seventh Street East, Bradenton, 34208; (941) 748-5829
Grove tours by tram, groveside café, orange juice wines, wildlife refuge (with gators), kids' play place and farm store. One of the most popular places in the state for the orange grove tourist to visit. Open since 1939.

South Naples Citrus Grove
341 Sabal Palm Road, Naples, FL 34114; (239) 774-3838
www.naplescitrus.com
Family owned and operated since 1979, right next to a grove. Fresh citrus, farm gifts, ice cream and key lime pies.

BIBLIOGRAPHY

All web sources in bibliography accessed in 2018.

GENERAL SOURCES

Attaway, John A. *A History of Florida Citrus Freezes*, DeLeon Springs: Florida Science Source, 1997.

Douglas, Marjory Stoneman. *Florida: The Long Frontier.* New York: Harper & Row, 1967.

Florida Citrus Hall of Fame. Various Entries. http://floridacitrushalloffame.com.

James, Beverly, Alec Richman, Brad Buck, Samantha Grenrock and Tom Nordlie. "A Look Back at 100 Years of Citrus Innovation." *Citrus Industry News,* June 2017. http://citrusindustry.net.

McPhee, John. *Oranges.* New York: Farrar, Straus and Giroux, 1967.

USDA Florida Citrus Reports. Various years. https://www.nass.usda.gov.

AN ORANGE GROVE, NOT AN ORCHARD

Pest Alert Plant Protection and Quarantine: Get the Facts on Citrus Greening (Huanglongbing). Animal and Plant Health Inspection Service Program Aid No. 1851. United States Department of Agriculture, June 2011.

Ruhl, Donna L. "Oranges and Wheat: Spanish Attempts at Agriculture in La Florida. In Diversity and Social Identity in Colonial Spanish America: Native American, African, and Hispanic Communities during the Middle Period." *Society for Historical Archaeology* 31, no. 1 (1997): 36–45.

A Way with Words. "Orchard vs. Grove," from "Blind Tiger" episode. Public radio program, February 27, 2015. https://www.waywordradio.org.

OLD ROOTS IN NORTHEAST FLORIDA

Bartram, William. *Travels through North & South Carolina, Georgia, East & West Florida, the Cherokee Country, the Extensive Territories of the Muscogulges, or Creek Confederacy, and the Country of the Chactaws.* Philadelphia, PA: James & Johnson, 1791.

Bohning, Gerry, and James A. Findlay. *Stories of Florida: Prepared for Use in Public Schools: A Selection of Original Writings from 1935–1943.* Fort Lauderdale, FL: Bienes Museum of the Modern Book, 2008.

Cresap, Ida Keeling. *The History of Florida Agriculture: The Early Era.* Florida Agricultural Experiment Station. Gainesville: University Press of Florida, 1982.

Fleszar, Mark J. "The Atlantic Mind: Zephaniah Kingsley, Slavery, and the Politics of Race in the Atlantic World." Thesis, Georgia State University, 2009.

Gold, Robert L. "That Infamous Floridian, Jesse Fish." *Florida Historical Quarterly* 52, no. 1 (1973): 1–17.

Harcourt, Helen. *Florida Fruits and How to Raise Them.* Louisville, KY: J.P. Morton and Company, 1886.

Herald St. Augustine. "The Mandarin Massacre." December 31, 1841.

Hooper, Kevin S. *The Early History of Clay County: A Wilderness that Could Be Tamed.* Charleston, SC: The History Press, 2006.

Lane, Marcia. "Dr. Garnett's Orange Grove Was a Fruitful Tourist Attraction." *St. Augustine Record*, September 23, 2013.

Moore, T.W., Reverend. *Treatise and Handbook of Orange Culture in Florida.* Jacksonville, FL: Ashmead Bros., 1881.

Rivers, Larry E. "A Troublesome Property: Master-Slave Relations in Florida, 1821–1865." In *The African American Heritage of Florida.* Edited by David R. Calburn and Jane L. Landers. Gainesville: University Press of Florida, 1995.

Schafer, Daniel L. *Anna Madgigine Jai Kingsley.* Gainesville: University Press of Florida, 2003.

Seminole Nation Museum. "The Seminole Wars." https://www.seminolenationmuseum.org.

Stowe, Charles E., and Lyman B. Stowe. *Harriet Beecher Stowe: The Story of Her Life.* Boston: Houghton Mifflin Company, 1911.

Stowe, Harriet Beecher. *Palmetto Leaves.* Gainesville: University Press of Florida, 1999.

Stowe, Harriet Beecher, John T. Foster and Sarah Whitmer Foster. *Calling Yankees to Florida: Harriet Beecher Stowe's Forgotten Tourist Articles.* Cocoa: Florida Historical Society Press, 2011.

Williams, Edwin L. "Negro Slavery in Florida." *Florida Historical Quarterly* 28, no. 2 (1949): 93–110.

UNSUNG HEROES OF THE GROVE

Amundson, Richard J. "Henry S. Sanford and Labor Problems in the Florida Orange Industry." *Florida Historical Quarterly* 43, no. 3 (1965): 229–43.

Florida Citrus Hall of Fame. "Dr. Philip Phillips." http://floridacitrushalloffame.com.

Meador, Paul. Interview with the author, April 2018.

Miller, S. "Interview by Oral History Team." The Contract Oral History Project, Libraries and Instructional Media Services. College of the Bahamas, Nassau, Bahamas, 1991.

Moore, K.C. "Marion County Florida: It's [*sic*] Agriculture and Horticulture." Marion County Chamber of Commerce, no date, estimated between 1923 and 1930.

Oliver, Kitty. Oral history interview with Dorothy McIntyre (Hollywood). Kitty Oliver Oral Histories: The Race and Change Project—Hollywood FL and Southern Broward County, 1999. http://digitalarchives.broward.org.

Rawlings, Marjorie Kinnan. *Cross Creek.* Reprint, New York: Scribner, 1996. Originally published in 1942.

Thompson, Tracey L. "Remembering 'The Contract': Recollections of Bahamians." *International Journal of Bahamian Studies* 18 (2012): 6–12.

Wood, Stan. Interview with the author, April 2018.

A SMALL RESURGENCE IN THE PANHANDLE

Andersen, Peter C. "UF/IFAS Evaluating Cold-Hardy Citrus Varieties for the Panhandle." *Panhandle Ag e-News*, February 17, 2017.

Moon, Troy. "Pensacola Nonprofit Will Pick Your Excess Fruit and Distribute It to the Needy." *Pensacola News Journal*, October 23, 2017.

"1928 Satsuma Orange Festival, Marianna, Florida." Filmstrip, UWF University Archives and West Florida History Center, 1928. https://archives.uwf.edu.

Pensacola News Journal, "Citrus Making a Comeback in Pensacola Area." December 3, 2013.

Rogers, Michael, Dr., President of the UF Citrus Research and Education Center. Interview with author, 2018.

Woods, Chuck. "Florida Panhandle Farmer Growing Satsuma Oranges as Alternative Crop." *Southeast Farm Press*, April 6, 2005.

CENTRAL AND NORTH CENTRAL: WHERE ORANGE WAS KING

Northern Edge, Ocala Area, Citra Pioneers, Pineapple Orange, Marion Today, Parson Brown

Brown, Mercer W. "The Parson Brown Orange." *Florida Historical Quarterly* 30, no. 1 (July 1951): 129–32.

Crosby, W.J. "Origin and Development of the Pineapple Orange." *Florida Horticultural Society Proceedings* 50 (1937): 129–30.

Florida Citrus Hall of Fame. "William J. Crosby" http://floridacitrushalloffame.com.

Flynn, Brenda. "McIntosh Thrives, but Quietly." *Ocala Star-Banner*, July 5, 2006.

Gainesville, Alachua County, Florida: The University City. Pamphlet. Gainesville, FL: Gainesville Chamber of Commerce, 1934.

Hand, Jen. "Attack of the Yellow Dragon." *Edible Northeast Florida* (January/February 2017).

Harris, John A. "History of the Orange Industry in Florida." *Florida State Horticultural Society Proceedings* 36 (1923): 205–15.

Kells, A.S. "Early Days at Citra." *Florida State Horticultural Society Proceedings* 31 (1918): 128–30.

Marks, Michael. "Don't Juice that Navel Orange!" *Mercury News*, October 29, 2014. https://www.mercurynews.com.

Mormino, Gary R. "The Enduring but Endangered Symbol of Florida." *Gainesville Sun*, April 3, 2016.

Palatka and Putnam County, Florida: Where Recreation and Industry Meet. Tampa, FL: Richard J. Amitage Company, 1967.

Soergel, Matt. "Putnam County Citrus Farm Hangs On, with Hard Work, Good Geography." *St. Augustine Record*, May 7, 2016.

Howey-in-the-Hills, Lake County Today

Beattie, Andrew. "The History of Insurance in America." Investopedia. https://www.investopedia.com.

Cohen, David. "Are Oranges Becoming Lake County Blues?" *Mount Dora Citizen*, July 17, 2015.

Fallstrom, Jerry. "Granddaughters Celebrate Town's Founder during Howey-in-the-Hills' Birthday Celebration." *Orlando Sentinel*, May 20, 2015.

Florida Citrus Hall of Fame. "Nick Faryna." http://floridacitrushalloffame.com.

Gillespie, Ryan. "Lake County Landmark's Next Chapter Begins at Sunsational Citrus in Umatilla." *Orlando Sentinel*, November 22, 2015.

Hughes, Melvin Edward, Jr. "William J. Howey and His Florida Dreams." *Florida Historical Quarterly* 66, No. 3 (January 1988): 243–64.

Ragavan, Chitra. "How a 1920s Florida Citrus Land Baron Created the Acid Test for Crypto Tokens." *Forbes* (November 14, 2017).

Secret Grove, Kissimmee, Osceola Today

Beauchamp, Catherine W. *Look What's Happened in Osceola County.* Kissimmee, FL: published for the Osceola County Art and Culture Center, 1983.

Cody, Aldus Morrill. *Osceola County: The First 100 Years.* Kissimmee, FL: Osceola County Historical Society, 1987.

Willson, Minnie Moore. *History of Osceola County: Florida Frontier Life.* Orlando, FL: Inland Press, 1935.

Sanford Experiment, Dr. Foster, Prince Butler Boston, Wheeler's Fertilizer, Seminole Today

Adams, Samuel Hawley. *Life of Henry Foster, M.D. Founder Clifton Springs Sanitarium*. Rochester, NY: Rochester Times-Union, 1921.

Adicks, Richard. *Oviedo: Biography of a Town*. Orlando, FL: Executive Press, 1979.

Canterbury Retreat. "Atkinson/Boston Family Files." http://www.canterburyretreat.org.

Florida Citrus Hall of Fame. "Benjamin Franklin Wheeler." http://floridacitrushalloffame.com.

———. "Harry Shelton Sandford." http://floridacitrushalloffame.com.

Robinson, Jim. "Boston's Dedication Bears Fruit in Community, Citrus Industry." *Orlando Sentinel*, February 2, 1989. Private collection of Ida Boston.

Some Account of Belair, Also of the City of Sanford Florida with a Brief Sketch of Their Founder. Pamphlet. Sanford, FL, 1889.

United States Federal Census. Alexander Atkinson, 1880. Census Place: Horse Stamp, Camden, GA; Roll 137, page 458C, Enumeration District 012.

Westgate, Phillip J. "Belair Groves, Sanford, Pioneer in Sub-Tropical Horticultural Introductions." *Florida Horticultural Society Proceedings* 66 (1953): 184–87.

The Ridge, Polk Sections, Griffin Orange Dynasty

Brown, Canter. *In the Midst of All that Makes Life Worth Living: Polk County, Florida, to 1940*. Tallahassee, FL: Sentry Press, 2001.

———. *None Can Have Richer Memories: Polk County, Florida, 1940–2000*. Tampa, FL: University of Tampa Press, 2005.

Florida Citrus Hall of Fame. "Ben Hill Griffin Jr." and "Ben Hill Griffin III." http://floridacitrushalloffame.com.

———. "Latimer 'Latt' Maxcy." http://floridacitrushalloffame.com.

Florida's Natural. "Ben Hill Griffin IV: Ben Hill Griffin, Inc." https://floridasnatural.com.

Florida Times-Union. Winter Haven Orange Festival articles. December 6, 1937; February 19, 1938.

Johnson, Charles. "Hunt Bros. Cooperative—Change Is a Vital Part of Their Business DNA." *Southeast Farm Press*, May 3, 2012.

Kohn, Keith W. "Drama Ends with Heirs Splitting Citrus Millions." *Orlando Sentinel*, August 17, 2003.

Marks, Rebeckah. "Frostproof: Small Town but Big History." *Polk County Historical Quarterly* 30, no. 3 (December 2003).

Morris, Robert A. *The U.S. Orange and Grapefruit Juice Markets: History, Development, Growth, and Change*. Gainesville: University of Florida Press, 2010.

Polk County Historical Quarterly (December 1976): 3.

Polk County Historical Quarterly (September 1974): 2.

Sharpe, Gaye Griffin. "'The Lake Wales Ridge Florida's Ancient Islands." *Naturally Central Florida*, 32–25. Joint venture between Orlando Economic Partnership (myregion.org) and the University of Central Florida's Metropolitan Center for Regional Studies.

Weekly, Carl W., Eric S. Menges and Roberta L. Pickert. "An Ecological Map of Florida's Lake Wales Ridge." *Florida Scientist* 71, no. 1 (2008): 45–64.

Orange County, Dr. Philip Phillips

Dickinson, Joy Wallace. "Doctor Phillips: The Real Deal." *Orlando Sentinel*. May 1, 2007. https://www.orlandosentinel.com.

Florida Citrus Hall of Fame. "Dr. Philip Phillips." http://floridacitrushalloffame.com.

Fruit Trade Journal and Produce Record 38 (1907): 22.

Kasab, Beth. "The End of Oranges in Orange County." *Orlando Sentinel*, April 27, 2016.

Southernmost Central Florida, Central Florida Past and Present

Florida Cattle Ranchers. "Doyle Carlton, III, Wauchula, Florida—Roman III Ranches." http://floridacattleranchers.com.

Florida Citrus Hall of Fame. "Joe L. Davis, Sr." http://floridacitrushalloffame.com.

Lowden, Jean F. *History of Hardee County*. Wauchula, FL, 1929.

Sunbelt Ag Expo. "C. Dennis Carlton Named 2014 Florida Farmer of the Year." July 14, 2014. http://sunbeltexpo.com.

SUNSHINE IN A GLASS

Birdsall, John. "The Orange Juice Boycott that Changed America." Extra Crispy—My Recipes, August 15, 2016. http://www.myrecipes.com/extracrispy.

Braun, Adee. "Misunderstanding Orange Juice as a Health Drink." *The Atlantic*, February 6, 2014.

Fetner, Tina, "Working Anita Bryant: The Impact of Christian Anti-Gay Activism on Lesbian and Gay Movement Claims." *Social Problems* 48, no. 3 (August 2001): 411–28.

Florida Citrus Hall of Fame. "Anita Bryant." http://floridacitrushalloffame.com.

Florida Statutes (2018), Chapter 601, Florida Citrus Code. Oxford University Press on behalf of the Society for the Study of Social Problems.

Funding Universe. "Company Histories Minute Maid." http://www.fundinguniverse.com.

———. "Company Histories Tropicana." http://www.fundinguniverse.com.

Hamilton, Alissa. *Squeezed: What You Don't Know About Orange Juice*. New Haven, CT: Yale University, 2009.

Hilltop Citrus. "History." http://www.hilltopcitrus.com.

Hojin's SW Orlando Real Estate Scoop. "Who in the World Is Dr. Phillips?" August 12, 2007. http://sworlandoblog.com.

Hughes, Melvin Edward, Jr. "William J. Howey and His Florida Dreams." *Florida Historical Quarterly* 66, no. 3 (January 1988): 243–64.

Mason, Carol. *Oklahoma: Lessons in Unqueering America*. New York: SUNY Press, 2015.

Modern Cities. "Where Your Florida Orange Juice Comes From." December 27, 2017. https://www.moderncities.com.

Osceola Fruit Distributors v. Mayo, 1959. Florida District Court of Appeals, So. 2d 760 115, page 763.

Polk County Historical Quarterly (September 1974): 3.

Rothaus, Steve. "Bob Green: Anita's Ex Paid Dearly in the Fight." *Miami Herald*, June 2007. http://miamiherald.typepad.com.

Rude, Emelyn. "The Surprising Link Between World War II and Frozen Orange Juice" *Time*, August 31, 2017. http://time.com.

Time. "Corporations: Minute Maid's Man." Monday, October 18, 1948. http://content.time.com.

U.S. Department of Agriculture. *Method of Preparing Full Flavored Fruit Juice Concentrates*. Louis G. MacDowell, Lakeland, and Edwin L. Moore and Cedric I. Atkins, Winter Haven, Florida, assignors to the United States of America as represented by the Secretary of Agriculture. Application August 7, 1945, serial no. 809,473, patent no. 2,453,109. Patented November 9, 1948.

Virgin, J.J. "Is Juice Really Worse than Soda?" *Huffington Post*, July 7, 2015. https://www.huffingtonpost.com.

Washington Post. "The Anita Bryant Show." March 2, 1977. https://www.washingtonpost.com.

Whirry, Robert. "Understanding Anita Bryant, the Woman Who Declared War on Gays" *The Advocate*, August 18, 2016.

YouTube. "Anita Bryant Confronted in 1977 (*Who's Who*) Interview." https://www.youtube.com.

———. "Anita Bryant Pie in the Face." https://www.youtube.com.

FIGURES AND HISTORY OF THE WEST COAST

DeFoor, J. Allison, II. *Odet Philippe: Peninsular Pioneer*. Safety Harbor, FL: Safety Harbor Museum of Regional History, 1997.

Dunedin Orange Festival. http://www.dunedinorangefestival.com/index.htm.

Florida Citrus Hall of Fame. "Dr. Karl Benjamin Albritton." http://floridacitrushalloffame.com.

———. "John S. Taylor." http://floridacitrushalloffame.com.

———. "Odet Philippe." http://floridacitrushalloffame.com.

———. "Ralph Burdick Polk." http://floridacitrushalloffame.com.

Gartner, Lisa. "Florida Scientists Are Working to Solve Greening. They Were Too Late for Cee Bee's." *Tampa Bay Times*, May 23, 2018.

Guerra, Melissa, and Eric Smithers. "Odet Philippe: The Story Behind the Namesake of Philippe Park in Safety Harbor." *South Tampa Magazine* (July 15, 2014).

Hakes, Ethel G. "The Romance of the Orange." *Florida Grower*, 1964. http://archive.wppl.org.

History of Hillsborough County. Federal Writers Project, July 25, 1936.

Oranges Online Buyers Guide. "Temple Oranges." https://www.orangesonline.com.

Salinero, Mike. "New Historic Marker Honors Temple Terrace Orange Grove History." 83 Degrees Media, February 2017. http://www.83degreesmedia.com.

Temple Terrace Preservation. "Bertha Potter Palmer." Terrace Preservation. http://www.templeterracepreservation.com.

LEGENDARY ORANGES OF CENTRAL EAST FLORIDA

Aronson, Virginia. *Gift of the Unicorn: The Story of Lue Gim Gong, Florida's Citrus Wizard.* Sarasota, FL: Pineapple Press, 2002.

Deland, Helen Parce. *Story of DeLand and Lake Helen, Florida.* Norwich, CT: Louis H. Walden, 1928.

Indian River Citrus League. "History." http://ircitrusleague.org.

Morton, J. "Orange." In *Fruits of Warm Climates.* Edited by Julia F. Morton. Miami, FL, 1987, 134–42. https://hort.purdue.edu.

Murray, Marian. *Plant Wizard: The Life of Lue Gim Gong.* Springfield, OH: Crowell-Collier Press, 1970.

Shipman, David. "The Citrus Wizard of Florida" USDA, May 16, 2012. https://www.usda.gov.

ON THE EDGE OF IT ALL IN SOUTHEAST FLORIDA

Atlantic Oceanographic and Meteorological Laboratory of NOAA. "Memorable Gulf Coast Hurricanes of the 20th Century." Updated 1993. http://www.aoml.noaa.gov.

Broward Digital Archives. "Broward County Historical Timeline Booklet." http://digitalarchives.broward.org.

Curl, Donald W. *Palm Beach County: An Illustrated History.* Northridge, CA: Windsor Publication, 1986.

Eklund, Christopher. "Citrus Demise? Land Developers Are Moving into Choice Broward Groves." *Ft. Lauderdale Sun-Sentinel,* November 5, 1980. Flamingo Gardens Archives, Davie, Florida.

"Flamingo Groves Gets Citrus Buds" Collect. 002.157, Ref. 001610. Flamingo Gardens Archives, Davie, Florida.

Fleshler, David. "Broward Homeowners to Get Millions for Lost Citrus." *Sun-Sentinel,* May 3, 2017.

———. "Homeowners Lose Citrus Canker Fight in Florida Supreme Court." *Sun-Sentinel,* July 13, 2017.

Fort Lauderdale Daily News. "Broward County Takes Stock of Storm Damage." September 22, 1947, 12. Flamingo Gardens Archives, Davie, Florida.

———. "Flamingo Groves Widely Known." March 11, 1929. Flamingo Gardens Archives, Davie, Florida.

Gillis, Susan. *Fort Lauderdale: The Venice of America.* Charleston, SC: Arcadia Publishing, 2004.

Gottwald, Tim R. (USDA, Agricultural Research Service, Fort Pierce, FL), James H. Graham (University of Florida, IFAS, Citrus Research and Education Center, Lake Alfred) and Tim S. Schubert, (Florida Department of Agriculture and Consumer Services, Division of Plant Industry, Gainesville). "Citrus Canker: The Pathogen and Its Impact." *American Phytopathological Society.* Peer reviewed by Plant Health Progress, accepted for publication July 17, 2002. https://www.freshfromflorida.com.

Hollingsworth, Tracy. *History of Dade County.* Coral Gables, FL: Glade House, 1949.

McGoun, Bill. *A Biographic History of Broward County.* Miami, FL: Miami Herald, 1972.

McIver, Stuart B. *Touched by the Sun.* Sarasota, FL: Pineapple Press, 2001.

Men Who Make Florida. Collect. 001.031, Ref. 006287, circa 1939. Flamingo Gardens Archives, Davie, Florida.

Mykle, Robert. *Killer 'Cane: The Deadly Hurricane of 1928.* New York: Cooper Square Press, 2002.

"Promoting Citrus Document," 2018. Flamingo Gardens Archives, Davie, Florida.

Roberts, H.J. *West Palm Beach Centennial Reflections.* West Palm Beach, FL: Sunshine Sentinel Press Inc., 1994.

"Selling Shares of the Grove." Collect. 002.140, Ref. 001587. Flamingo Gardens Archives, Davie, Florida.

Stirling, Frank. "Citrus Growing on the Muck Soils." *Florida Horticultural Society Proceedings* 41 (1928): 31–34. Flamingo Gardens Archives, Davie, Florida.

St. Petersburg Times. "Pinellas Weathers Hurricane with Only Minor Damage." September 19, 1947, 15.

Turner, Gregg. *A Journey into Florida Railroad History.* Gainesville: University Press of Florida, 2008.

———. *A Short History of Florida's Railroads.* Charleston, SC: Arcadia Publishing, 2003.

Vickers, Raymond B. *Panic in Paradise: Florida's Banking Crash of 1926.* Tuscaloosa: University of Alabama Press, 1994.

Wagner, Victoria. "The Davie Dilemma." Town of Davie, 1982. https://www.davie-fl.gov.

Walter, Sidney. *Florida's Flagler.* Athens: University of Georgia Press, 1949.

Wood, Stan. Interview with the author, April 2018.

CHALLENGES

Dewdney, Megan. Interview with the author, 2018.

Gmitter, Fred. Interview with the author, 2018.

Grosser, Jude. Interview with the author, 2018.

Murphy, Michael Joe. "Citrus Greening: Will a Signature Industry for Florida Survive?" *Orlando Sentinel*, June 15, 2017. Digital Conversation Starter. https://www.orlandosentinel.com.

Rogers, Michael. Interview with the author, 2018.

Ruane, Laura Patrick. "Citrus Industry Looks for Help to Turn the Corner on Citrus Greening Fight," News-press.com, part of the USA Today Network, June 9, 2017. https://www.news-press.com.

Satran, Joe. "Citrus Greening Forces Florida Growers to Trust a Controversial Savior." *Huffington Post*, August 30, 2013. https://www.huffingtonpost.com.

UF/IFAS News. "UF Sugar Belle Citrus Variety More Tolerant to Greening." May 19, 2017. http://nwdistrict.ifas.ufl.edu.

SOUTHWEST FLORIDA: THE NEW CENTER OF ORANGES

Meador, Paul. Interview with the author, April 2018.

Saunders, Kathy. "The Citrus Place, One of the Last Holdouts in Independent Florida Citrus, Is Serving Up Fresh Juice in Terra Ceia." *Tampa Bay Times*, March 20, 2017. http://www.tampabay.com.

INDEX

ABOUT THE AUTHOR

 **E** rin Thursby is a founding member and executive director of GastroJax, a nonprofit promoting North Florida food, beverage and food education and host of the food fest GastroFest in Jacksonville, Florida. She's also a regular freelance writer for local publications in Jacksonville, including *Edible Northeast Florida*, and is food editor for *EU Jacksonville*. She's lived in Florida all her life and is a graduate of the University of South Florida.

Visit us at
www.historypress.com